Understanding JESUS' TEACHINGS

Don Wettlaufer

outskirtspress
DENVER, COLORADO

Understanding Jesus' Teachings
All Rights Reserved.
Copyright © 2013 Don Wettlaufer
v3.0

Outskirts Press, Inc.
http://www.outskirtspress.com

ISBN: 978-1-4787-0413-3

Outskirts Press and the "OP" logo are trademarks belonging to Outskirts Press, Inc.

PRINTED IN THE UNITED STATES OF AMERICA

This book is dedicated to my teachers:

Tim H., Terry M., Bobby P., Peter H., Al M., Paul O., and John B.

and to all those who have a desire to know God's word

Caution! This book will explain the teachings of Jesus. After reading it, you will know clearly what Jesus desires from His followers. What you do with that information is up to you. However, you should know that what you do, or do not do, with it may impact you for eternity.

Introduction

God gets our attention in numerous ways, some subtle and some overt. Regardless how He got your attention, what He wants is a personal relationship with you. Yes, believe it or not, the God who created the universe wants to communicate with you, and fellowship with you, and to show you how much He loves you.

This book is designed to draw you into a relationship with the one true God. It will talk about heaven and hell, our enemy the devil, and our savior Jesus. It will talk about all the really cool benefits of being a follower of Jesus, as well as the tactics the devil will use to try to trip you up. It will teach you how to communicate with God, how to keep the devil and his curses out of your life, how to keep your focus on the next life, rather than living for the present world, and how the Holy Spirit can empower you to get on fire to do God's work on earth. It will conclude with the rise of the Antichrist and the "end times" tribulation and how you can be spared those terrible times that lay ahead.

This book is designed to make disciples for Jesus. It will help you to understand the major themes of the Bible so you can understand God's purpose. Ideally, you should have a partner to go through this book with you, one who can pray with you, encourage you, and discuss the things God is speaking to you.

This book may open your eyes to some things you may have been doing which are displeasing to God and make you aware of some things you should be doing that you are not. This book is not meant to be another set of rules for how you are to live. It is not a yoke that God is placing over your shoulders to burden you. It is meant to teach you how you can have true happiness and be one with the Most High God. As God speaks to you personally about things He wants you to change, jot them down in the appendix. Be praying about life change, asking God for the power to make it happen. Revisit the list periodically to see if God is making any changes in you. I think you will be pleasantly surprised. I think others in your life who are close to you will also notice changes in you.

This book will help you apply the things you are learning. At the end of each section are application questions. These will help you reflect on what you have just read and help give you the resolve to implement some meaningful changes in your life. There will be memory verses throughout the book to help cement God's truths in your life. Memorize these verses. Meditate on all the verses you encounter in this book. Underline them in your Bible. Write in the margins of your Bible any explanation that is new to you. God is starting a new and wonderful work in your life. He intends to carry it through to completion, as promised in Philippians 1:6, and to transform your life. *"Being confident of this, that he who began a good work in you will carry it on to completion until the day of Christ Jesus."*

Contents

Week 1

To Whom Are You Going to Listen?

When someone tells me about their religious beliefs, and it sounds different from what the Bible has to say, I ask them, "On what are you basing your information?" There's a lot of misinformation floating out there that's based on what our culture has to say or maybe what our friends tell us. So, to whom should you listen? When you have questions about God, heaven and hell, how to get to heaven, or about the devil, you could ask a friend who has no first-hand knowledge of these things, or you could consult with Jesus, who came from heaven, knows the devil, and resides at the right hand of God.

Why should we believe Jesus?

Jesus was a miracle worker. He performed miracles that ranged from healing the blind and lame, to driving out demons, to raising people from the dead.

Jesus was a prophet. He foretold the destruction of Jerusalem, which happened 40 years after Jesus' crucifixion, and foretold of his own death and resurrection.

Jesus was able to read people's minds and address what they were thinking.

Jesus taught people about the Kingdom of God. People observed that He spoke with authority and they were amazed.

Jesus was without sin. Even Pilate admitted, at the trial of Jesus, "this man has done nothing wrong."

When Jesus and the disciples were out on a boat and caught in a storm, Jesus spoke to the wind and waves and calmed the seas.

Demons obeyed Him.

Jesus walked on water.

Jesus' life fulfilled over 200 Old Testament prophecies about Himself that were written as much as a thousand years before He walked the earth. His death by crucifixion was predicted in Psalm 22. His being born in Bethlehem was predicted in Micah 5:2. His being born of a virgin was predicted in Isaiah 7:14. His suffering for our sins was predicted in Isaiah 53:5,10.

Jesus rose from the dead and appeared to hundreds of eyewitnesses in the 40 days after His resurrection. Even the religious leaders of that time, who did not believe His claims to be the Son of God, admitted that He was sent by God.

Clearly Jesus was no ordinary man. So when it comes to believing what the world tells me or what Jesus tells me, I have to believe Jesus. His life is thoroughly documented in the first four books of the New Testament: Matthew, Mark, Luke, and John.

Trust the Bible Completely
Read It

Many people want to know if the bible can be trusted. 2 Timothy 3:16 says, *"All scripture is God-breathed."* This means that through the Holy Spirit, God put His thoughts into the minds of the authors who wrote the bible so that they documented what God wanted to say to us. 2 Peter 1:21 says, *"Men spoke from God as they were carried along by the Holy Spirit."* Jesus said when speaking to God in John 17:17, *"Your word is truth,"* and instructed that we are sanctified (set apart) by the word. Jesus also said in Matthew 24:35, *"Heaven and earth will pass away, but my words will never pass away."* So yes, you can trust it. In fact, the Bible is a living document, since God speaks to us when we read it and when we meditate on what it has to say. *"The word of God is living and active,"* says Hebrews 4:12. *"Sharper than any double-edged sword, it penetrates even to dividing soul and spirit, joints and marrow; it judges the thoughts and attitudes of the heart."* That's a pretty compelling book review. Other Bible authors said it sets you free (John 8:32), it is enlightening (Psalm 119:105), it helps you to not sin (Psalm 119:11) and it has the power to lead to salvation (Romans 1:16). God, speaking through the prophet Isaiah, said in Isaiah 55:11, *"My word that goes out from my mouth will not return to me empty, but will accomplish what I desire and achieve the purpose for which I sent it."* When God speaks to you through His word, His word acts upon you with its transforming power and fulfills the purpose for which God gave it to you, whether it was to inform you, warn you, train you, act upon your heart to change you, and so on.

Believe It

When you read it, you must believe it. Often, people decide that some parts of the Bible are folklore or legend and can't be taken literally. Even in Jesus' day, people struggled with the validity of Noah building an ark and rescuing two of every kind of animal, or Jonah being alive in the belly of a whale for three days. But Jesus made reference to both of these Bible stories (Luke 17:26 and Luke 11:30) giving credence to the fact that they were real events. Other people may decide that, based on today's culture, certain parts of the Bible are irrelevant to today's living, and should be disregarded. Too many people pick and choose what they want to believe and fill in the blanks with something from the world's belief system, thereby forming their own version of Christianity. This is not only dangerous, but it is arrogant and offensive to God. It points to a lack of complete submission to God. You will find that when you make a decision to trust every bit of the Bible, that God will then reveal more of His word to you. When you start to believe all that the Bible has to say, you will observe that God is working in you to change you. 1 Thessalonians 2:13 says, *"And we also thank God continually because, when you received the word of God, which you heard from us, you accepted it not as the word of men, but as it actually is, the word of God, <u>which is at work in you who believe</u>."*

Key Principle: The degree to which you dig deep into the word and believe what it says determines the degree to which God opens it up to you.

Jesus said in Mark 4:24, *"Consider carefully what you hear. With the measure you use, it will be measured to you. Whoever has, will be given more; whoever does not have, even what he has will be taken from him."* If you search for the truth with all your being, God will reward your search and fill you with discoveries in His word. If your search for the truth is casual and superficial, God may reveal less of Himself to you. Put another way: Open up to God, and He will open up to you. But don't take the quest seriously, and God will not take you seriously. Jeremiah 29:13 says, *"You will seek me and find me when you seek me with all your heart."*

Apply It
Key Principle: It does you no good to study the word unless you apply it to your life.
Read the following two short passages: Luke 6:46-49 and James 1:22-25.

In the first passage, Jesus finds fault with those who claim to be followers of Jesus, yet their lives look nothing like His. He states that this kind of living leads to destruction in the end.

In the second passage, James, the brother of Jesus, tells us that merely listening to the word, without doing what it says, leads to deceiving ourselves. It is like waking up in the morning and looking in the mirror and seeing your hair is a mess, you need to shave or put on makeup, and you have morning breath, but instead of making yourself presentable, you get dressed for work, forgetting what you look like. That would be crazy! But it's equally crazy to read about how you should be living your life, yet do nothing about it.

APPLICATION:

You may discover that some things in the Bible are just too hard to do. Don't get discouraged. Jesus said in Matthew 19:26, *"With man this is impossible, but with God all things are possible."*

1. What areas of the Bible seem most difficult to believe? Will you take a step of faith and decide that going forward you will believe the Bible completely?
2. Will you decide to really dig into this book and give it a passionate effort to learn what God has to say to you? Remember, to the degree you really search for the truth determines the degree to which God reveals it to you.
3. I invite you to write down in the appendix those things God is revealing to you so far, and ask God to help you apply them to your life.

Memory Verse:

Philippians 1:6 *"Being confident of this, that he who began a good work in you will carry it on to completion until the day of Christ Jesus."*

It Is Not About You; It Is About Him

So now that God has my attention, what is it He wants from me? As Rick Warren says in his book, <u>The Purpose Driven Life</u>, "It's not about you. The God of the universe created you for His purpose." [1] He didn't just create you and say, "Go have a good time, enjoy yourself." The world tells us to make a lot of money and buy a lot of stuff, and when you fill up your house, go buy a bigger one so you can have room for more stuff. Then go and spend all your money on yourself, seeking all the entertainment and pleasure you can stand. The one who dies with the most "stuff" wins. But the Bible says we should first seek to know God. John 17:3 tells us eternal life is all about having a relationship with God, knowing Him personally, and His son Jesus Christ, and giving God first place in our lives. Secondly, we should understand <u>His</u> will for our lives (Ephesians 5:17).

Could it be you've been misled all this time? That life is <u>not</u> all about success, fame, status, achievement, popularity, money, and power? Rather, it's about having a relationship with the God who loves you so much that He watched His only Son be nailed to a cross so that your sins would not be counted against you. And it's about honoring what Jesus did for you by serving Him, according to how God wants you to serve.

God gave His laws, the Ten Commandments, to Moses and etched them in stone tablets (Exodus 20). The first four have to do with loving

God with all your heart, soul, mind, and strength: not worshipping anyone or anything besides God, not worshipping idols, not using God's holy name as a slang word or curse, and honoring God's day (Sunday) by keeping it holy, that is, not laboring over the work you do the other days of the week. The fifth commandment is about honoring your parents, doing what they ask without opposition and defiance. The last five commandments have to do with loving your neighbor and are necessary to get along: don't kill your neighbor, don't rip him off, don't lie to him, don't desire your neighbor's wife, and don't desire your neighbor's stuff. The big ten can be summarized like this: Love God and love others.

Love God

Jesus said in Mark 12:30, that the way to start having a relationship with God is to *"Love the Lord your God with all your heart and with all your soul and with all your mind and with all your strength."* The Bible calls this the "greatest commandment." God wants to be your greatest passion, your first love, your foremost relationship. He wants to hear from you when you wake up and lie down, when you're in trouble, or when you're just enjoying His creation, when you need healing, and when you're feeling great. He wants you to love what He loves and hate what He hates. He longs to have a relationship with you.

God desires praise. Revelation 5:11 tells us there are 100 million angels encircling God's throne singing praises. Yes, God wants you to add your voice to their number.

God desires obedience. Jesus said in John 14:23 regarding obedience, *"If anyone loves me, he will obey my teaching. My Father will love him, and we will come to him and make our home with him."* So we can show our love of God by praising Him and obeying His commands.

Key Principle: Complete obedience results in God's blessings.
Read Deuteronomy, chapter 28.

God takes pleasure in giving you gifts. While God's love for you is unconditional, His blessings are conditional. He desires your obedience to His laws. You may ask, "Why can't He just give us the gifts with no strings attached?" Someone else already does that—Santa Claus. But God is not Santa Claus. Like a parent who knows what is best for his child, He rewards good behavior and punishes bad behavior. In Deuteronomy 28, God makes a promise with His chosen nation of Israel, the people Moses led out of slavery in Egypt. He promises that if they carefully obey all His commands, He will bless them abundantly. He will set their nation above all nations on earth, their children will be blessed, their work will be blessed, they will be prosperous and thrive, their enemies will be defeated, and they will be blessed with abundant rain.

But if they don't obey all His commands, they will be cursed. Their land will be cursed, their children cursed, and their work will be cursed until they come to ruin. They will be plagued with diseases. They will be defeated by their enemies. Their homes, possessions, and children will be taken over by another nation. They will be unsuccessful in everything they do, and day after day they will be oppressed and robbed. Their food will be devoured by pests. Aliens (foreigners) who live among them will rise up to rule over them.

The people of Israel chose not to obey God's commands and their nation was cursed. Since God does not change (Malachi 3:6), you can be assured that the same blessings, curses, and conditions apply to His people today, just as they did 3500 years ago. Jesus said in John 14:21, *"Whoever has my commands and obeys them, he is the one who loves me."* Obey God's laws and begin to find favor with the Most High.

APPLICATION:
Read Matthew 21:28-32, the parable of the obedient son.

What is the meaning of this parable? The meaning is this: that some people say 'Yes' to God but then do not obey Him. Good intentions are one thing, but only by your actions can you show true obedience.

1. If you loved golfing so much that it interfered with your being

able to go to church on Sunday mornings, would you be putting God first in your life?

2. Do you think that God desires worship on Sunday only?
    Some people say they just don't get anything out of going to
    church. Consider this: you are not there just to get something,
    you are there to give something. You are there to give honor
    to God and give Him your worship.
3. Has God laid on your heart any area in which you need to
    change? Have you learned something new? Write these down
    in the appendix.
4. God longs to pour out His blessings on you. But you must be
    completely obedient to following His commands.

Memory Verse:

John 17:3 *"Now this is eternal life: that they may know you, the
only true God, and Jesus Christ, whom you have sent."*

Love Others

Read Matthew 25:34-40.

The second greatest commandment is to love your neighbor as yourself (Mark 12:31). In Matthew 25:34-40, Jesus personalized this command by saying that whenever you fed the hungry, gave water to the thirsty, took in a stranger, clothed the naked, took care of the sick, or visited those in prison, you actually did it to Him. So the foremost way to show your love of Jesus, and to serve Him, is to take care of the needy of this world. In Deuteronomy 28:47-48, God warns that if you do not serve the Lord joyfully and gladly in the time of your prosperity, then you will serve your enemies in dire poverty and hunger. So those who have been blessed by God are required to be a blessing to others. 1 John 4:12 says, *"If we love one another, God lives in us and his love is made complete in us."*

Key Principle: God is glorified when his church acts as the hands and feet of Christ to those in need.
Read Mark 10:42-45.

Whoever wants to become great, must be a slave to all. James, the brother of Jesus, taught in James 2:15-16, *"Suppose a brother or sister is without clothes and daily food. If one of you says to him, 'Go, I wish you well; keep warm and well fed,' but does nothing about his physical needs, what good is it?"* So we really serve others when we act out of compassion to meet their needs, not just wish them well. Jesus said in John 13:35 regarding loving others, *"By this all men will know that you are my disciples, if you love one another."* He intended for Christians to be known by their love for others, not for their keeping of the law, upholding their morality, or appearing religious. When others see your acts of compassion for the needy, they will marvel at what love exists among Christians for one another. Matthew 5:16 says, *"Let your light shine before men, that they may see your good deeds and praise your Father in heaven."*

Paul taught in Galatians 6:10, *"Therefore, as we have opportunity, let us do good to all people, especially to those who belong to the family of believers."* So our first acts of compassion should be toward other believers. But Jesus taught even to *"Love your enemies, do good to them...Then your reward will be great, and you will be sons of the Most High"* (Luke 6:35). Love my enemies? Really? That's too hard! But consider that God loved us even while we were still sinners (Romans 5:8), not after we cleaned up our act and decided to become a follower of Him. While we were enslaved to sin and turning away from God, He gave the ultimate gift of His Son's life to bring us back to Him. When you consider that God loves you unconditionally, you will begin to have His heart, and to love whom He loves. When people encounter the unconditional love of God, they are forever changed.

Read Luke 10:30-37, the parable of the Good Samaritan.

In this story, two religious men, a priest and a Levite, did nothing to help the Jewish man who was beaten and robbed. They probably said a prayer for him under their breath and maybe wished him well, and then went on their way. But it was a Samaritan, a Gentile who was despised by the Jews, (an enemy, you could say) who came to the man's aid and took action out of compassion for him. The disciple John taught, in

The disciple John taught, in 1 John 3:17-18, *"If anyone has material possessions and sees his brother in need but has no pity on him, how can the love of God be in him? Dear children, let us not love with words or tongue but with actions and in truth."*

APPLICATION:

1. Would you ask God to show you a way to regularly feed the hungry, clothe the needy, visit the incarcerated, or take care of the sick? When He answers you, record your answer in the appendix.

2. When you do something to show your love for others, you are to give God the glory, and not glorify yourself. In Galatians 1:10 the apostle Paul asked the question, *"Am I now trying to win the approval of men, or of God? Or am I trying to please men? If I were still trying to please men, I would not be a servant of Christ."* In Matthew 6:1, Jesus said, *"Be careful not to do your acts of righteousness before men, to be seen by them. If you do, you will have no reward from your Father in heaven."* How can you ensure God gets the glory and not you?

3. When is the last time you saw a complete stranger in need? What did you do for him/her? When is the last time you saw a believer in need? Was your response any different?

4. Record in the appendix what God is telling you through this lesson.

Memory Verse:

Romans 5:8 *"But God demonstrates his own love for us in this: While we were still sinners, Christ died for us."*

After Death, Judgment

Key Principle: God will evaluate how we lived our lives while on earth.

As Francis Chan so clearly explains in his "Youtube" video, "Just Stop and Think", the Bible tells us that one day, we will all stand before God and be judged. You may look at evil people in the world and think, "I will do okay, I am not as bad as they are." But God does not compare us to people who may be worse than us. He does not grade us on a curve. Instead, He compares us to His laws. And if you are honest, you will realize you are going to be found guilty of breaking His laws.[2] Spoken another way, the bible says in Isaiah 53:6, *"each of us has turned to his own way."* We have rebelled from following God's ways.

Key Principle: Sin results in spiritual death.

Just as God created physical laws, like gravity, inertia, momentum, and centrifugal force, he also created spiritual laws. Laws such as "You reap what you sow," and "Whoever humbles himself will be exalted." One such law is referred to in Romans 8:2, the "law of sin and death." It is explained in Romans 6:23 this way: *The wages of* (or payment for) *our sin is death.* Since God does not create a law and then later make exceptions to it, He is completely justified in punishing us for our sin with spiritual death (eternal separation from God in hell). But here's the key truth of the matter: God doesn't want to punish us.[3] He made a way out for us by having His Son, Jesus, take our punishment (through His death on a cross). Since Jesus died for us, we don't have to die. He has already paid our penalty of death. Now we can live with God for eternity in heaven. *"Christ redeemed us from the curse of the law by becoming a curse for us."* (Galatians 3:13). We were redeemed (bought and paid for) through the shedding of His blood, and therefore we belong to Him.

Can you imagine having to watch someone you love be nailed to a cross and hang there until he dies? Yet God asked His only Son to endure the agony of the cross. Jesus did so willingly, that we might stand before God as innocent people, not guilty of sin which results in death, but washed clean of our sin by the blood of Jesus. What an amazing, amazing love story. It's hard to imagine that God loves us that much.

APPLICATION:

1. What do you call a leader or king who makes a rule and then holds everyone accountable to it, with no exceptions and without showing favoritism?
2. What do you call a leader or king who upholds the rules but goes to tremendous lengths to ensure we don't have to take the punishment for breaking the rule by inflicting the punishment on himself instead?
3. Is that just the most incredible thing imaginable?

Memory Verse:

Romans 6:23 *"For the wages of sin is death, but the gift of God is eternal life in Christ Jesus our Lord."*

Heaven

Read Revelation chapters 4 and 5.

Since Jesus made it possible for us to be with Him in Heaven, let's talk about what the Bible has to say about Heaven. Heaven was discussed frequently by Jesus. The bible says we will do three things in Heaven.

First, we will worship God. In the book of Revelation, the apostle John is shown, by Jesus, a picture of what is going on in Heaven. In Revelation chapters 4 and 5, we see an incredible picture of the worship that is taking place. A king is sitting on His throne and He's glowing like precious stones. A rainbow encircles the throne. Around the throne are twenty-four other thrones. Seated on the thrones are twenty-four elders, dressed in white with crowns of gold on their heads. There is thunder and lightning coming from the center throne. There are four creatures with six wings hovering around the center throne, crying out, "Holy, holy, holy is the Lord God Almighty." One hundred million angels are shouting, "Worthy is the Lamb!" Then, every creature in Heaven and on earth, and even under the earth (Hell) are praising Jesus and falling down to worship Him. This is a fulfillment of the prophecy in Philippians 2:10, *"That at the name of Jesus every knee should bow, in heaven and on earth and under the earth, and every tongue confess that Jesus Christ is Lord, to the glory of God the Father."*

Secondly, the Bible says we will have some kind of work to do serving God. Revelation 22:3 says, *"His servants will serve Him."* God ordained work such that when man is working, he feels fulfilled. God even gave Adam work to do in the Garden of Eden. The same verse also says, *"No longer will there be any curse."* This refers to God's curse of man's work in Genesis 3:17-19. When Adam sinned in the Garden of Eden by disobeying God, God cursed his work. He said man would only eat after painful toil and after competing with weeds and pests in order to get food out of the ground. We would become frustrated because things would not work right the first time, other things would fall apart, and along the way, the second law of thermodynamics would turn everything toward decay and disorder. But in Heaven, the curse is lifted. So man's work will be rewarding, productive, and efficient. What he builds will last, things will go right the first time, and he will not be frustrated by failure along the way.

The third thing we will do in Heaven is experience great pleasure and wondrous things. 1 Corinthians 2:9 says, *"No eye has seen, no ear has heard, no mind has conceived what God has prepared for those who love him."* And Psalm 16:11 says God will fill us *"with eternal pleasures at your right hand."* To help experience this wonderful place, God will give us a new physical body. 1 Corinthians 15:42 tells us it will be an imperishable body, it will not know decay. Philippians 3:21 says Jesus *"will transform our lowly bodies so that they will be like his glorious body."* So what was Jesus' post-resurrection, glorious body like? For one thing, Jesus could teleport his body wherever he wanted to go. "Startrek" fans take note. In John 20:19 the disciples were in a room with the doors locked and Jesus suddenly appeared in the room. In Luke 24:13-31, Jesus appeared next to two disciples who were on the road to Emmaus. They were kept from recognizing Him. He stayed with them, explaining all the events of the crucifixion and resurrection to them. Then, after their eyes were opened and they realized they were talking with Jesus, he disappeared from their sight. 1 Corinthians 15:44 tells us that instead of having a natural body, we will have a spiritual body. In other words, we won't be ruled by the desires of the flesh, but our bodies will be governed through the Holy Spirit. Praise God! Certainly our bodies will have no physical handicaps. If you suffer with a disability on earth, you will rejoice in your new, disease-free body in Heaven. Perhaps the greatest promise of all is found in 1 John 3:2, *"...when he appears, we shall be like him, for we shall see him as he is."* It should be the goal and pursuit of every believer to strive to become like Jesus while we're living on earth. Jesus expects us to be continually making progress with that goal in mind. But in the end, Jesus will complete the transformation and we will become fully like Christ; not that we will be deity but we will have His love for the Father and His love for each other. We will be totally without sin. We will overflow with worship and service to our God.

Next, we will be able to enjoy food in Heaven. John 21:9-12 tells of Jesus' cooking fish on the shore and when the disciples came in from fishing, he invited them to have breakfast with him. Luke 13:29 and Luke 14:15 even talks about a banquet celebration that takes place in heaven. Isaiah 25:6 describes it as a feast of rich food for all peoples, the best of meats and the finest of wines.

In his book <u>Heaven</u>, Randy Alcorn suggests we will probably have enhanced senses. We may be able to see in more colors, hear more frequencies, smell more aromas, see further distances, and experience enhanced taste buds.[4]

Revelation 21:4 tells us, *"There will be no more death, or mourning, or crying, or pain."* Loved ones won't be taken from us through disease, suffering, and old age. We will experience no adversity, discouragement, hurt, rejection, emotional wounds, or physical distress. Heaven will be a place of healing. God Himself will wipe away every tear and pour healing salve on our wounds.

The New Jerusalem
Read Revelation 21:1-3 and Revelation 21:10-22:5

These passages tell us the current earth will one day cease to exist. God will create a new Heaven and a new earth. Then He will lower from Heaven, onto the new earth, a city, the New Jerusalem. It will be God's home, where He dwells with His people. The city will shine with the brilliance of a diamond sparkling in sunlight. It will be the radiance of God's glory that gives it light. It will be a city of unimaginable beauty, made of gold, jewels, and precious stones. The gates will be made of pearl and the streets paved with gold. Chapter 21, verse 16 even gives the dimensions of the new city. It will measure 12,000 stadia in length, and be as wide and high as it is long. So it will either be cube shaped or pyramid shaped. Converted into miles, it will be large enough to span from Maine to Florida and from the east coast to the Rocky Mountains. It will be as high as it is long, so there will be more than enough room to house all the resurrected believers from all time. A river of crystal clear water will flow down the middle of the city, originating from the throne of God. It will be a reminder that Jesus is the source of living water. On either side of the river will stand a "Tree of Life." This tree was first mentioned as being in the Garden of Eden, along with the Tree of the Knowledge of Good and Evil. Adam and Eve were driven from the garden after they sinned so they would not eat of the Tree of Life. But now man will be free to eat its leaves, which will provide healing.

Most wondrous of all, we will live in the presence of God. Revelation 22:4 says, *"They will see His face and His name will be on their foreheads."* We will see God in all His glory, which no man on earth has ever done. God told Moses in Exodus 33:20 that no one can see His face and live. It's only because we have been made holy and are now sinless that we will be able to see God in His full glory and live. We also will see our Savior, Jesus Christ, sitting at the right hand of God (Mark 14:62). We will see Him as man, to remind us of Jesus' obedience in leaving the glory of heaven to take on the form of a man (Philippians 2:7) and at times, like a lamb on a throne (Revelation 5:6), signifying His role as the Holy Lamb of God, the sacrifice for sin. Jesus said in John 17:24, when speaking about His followers, that He longs to have us with Him in His heavenly home and for us to see Him in all His glory.

More than simply seeing God, the apostle Paul tells us we will also share in His glory (Romans 8:18 and 2 Corinthians 4:17). What a transformation that will be! It may possibly be like Jesus' transfiguration on the mountain, where Jesus gave his disciples a glimpse of His coming glory. *"His face shone like the sun, and his clothes became as white as the light,"* it says in Matthew 17:2. Maybe that's what Jesus was referring to in Revelation 3:4, *"They will walk with me, dressed in white, for they are worthy."*

How much fun will it be to sing, dance, walk, and laugh with Jesus? In heaven, we will see Jesus' servant nature. Isaiah 25:6 tells us Jesus will prepare the banquet feast. Jesus may have been talking about himself when he described the faithful servant in Luke 12:37, *"...He will dress himself to serve, will have them recline at the table, and will come and wait on them."* What a welcoming reception He will throw for us!

Heaven won't be a place where we float around on clouds, like spirits, playing harps. We will live in a physical existence with a physical body, finding significance in our work, praising God and never tiring of it, constantly exploring and experiencing new wonders. It will be a place of security, devoid of sin, where we engage in perfect relationships with one another. We will be eternally happy and satisfied.

The Bible closes with a picture of Heaven in order to give us an eternal perspective of our life on earth. Earth is not our final destination. We are only here temporarily. We are destined for a much better place. So don't pursue the things of this world, rather, pursue the kingdom of God.

APPLICATION:

1. What is the most exciting thing to you about Heaven?
2. If you are to live in the Heaven described above, what one thing about you will have to be changed the most?
3. Are you going?

Memory Verse:

Philippians 2:10-11 *"That at the name of Jesus every knee should bow, in heaven and on earth and under the earth, and every tongue confess that Jesus Christ is Lord, to the glory of God the Father."*

Hell

Read Luke 16:19-31.

Although the majority of people who call themselves Christians believe in Heaven, far fewer believe in Hell. However, Jesus spoke about Hell repeatedly. He gave His longest monologue about Hell in the parable of Lazarus and the rich man. Read Luke 16:19-31.

In this story, the rich man winds up in Hell for (among other reasons) ignoring the plight of Lazarus, a beggar who camped out at the gate of the rich man, hoping for some scraps of food. The rich man cries out to Abraham, whom he sees in Paradise. He asks for water to cool his tongue because he is in <u>agony</u> in the fire. He is told by Abraham that the chasm between Heaven and Hell is impossible to cross, so there is no escaping Hell, and likewise no one can come down to visit him to provide relief. The rich man refers to Hell as a place of torment. Jesus painted a scene where those in Hell have a physical body and experience extreme suffering. In Mark 9:48, it is described as a place where the fire is not quenched and the worm (that is eating away at your physical body) does not die. Thirst, heat, agony, torment, suffering. That's how Jesus described Hell.

Like Heaven, in Hell people will have a physical body that most likely has enhanced senses. The pain, the heat, and the thirst will be all the more acute. Some have likened Hell to being in a steam room. When the steam is cranked up, you have an awareness of other people being in the room, although you can't make out their faces. You would like to have a conversation, but when you open your mouth, the heat burns your mouth and throat. After a few minutes, you don't feel like socializing with anyone. You want to exit the steam room in a hurry. But in Hell, you can not exit. Your suffering is for all eternity.

In Matthew 8:12, Jesus talked about people being thrown *"into the darkness, where there will be weeping and gnashing of teeth."* The weeping will be for themselves, while they recall all the times they rejected Jesus and all the times they lived for themselves, passing on opportunities to help others. The gnashing of teeth will be directed at God, for condemning them to eternal torment.

Jesus said in Matthew 25:41 that Hell was *"prepared for the devil and his angels,"* those angels who were banished from heaven, along with Satan, when they rebelled against God (see Revelation 12:9). However, God wouldn't be a just God if only evil angels wound up there and not evil people. He wouldn't be a just God if he gave a lesser punishment for rebellion by humans than for rebellion by angels. Jesus said Hell is real.

APPLICATION:

1. How would you feel if, while standing in hell, you remembered you had the road map to heaven sitting right in front of you in the form of this book, but did not take the time to read the book? Will you take the time to complete this book? It may impact your eternity.

Memory Verse:

Matthew 10:28 *"Do not be afraid of those who kill the body but cannot kill the soul. Rather, be afraid of the One who can destroy both soul and body in hell."*

Week 2

Satan

Who is Satan?

There are two passages in the Old Testament that identify Satan (who was called Lucifer).

Ezekiel 28:12-17 tells the following: *"You were the model of perfection, full of wisdom and perfect in beauty."* If it's possible for God to derive more joy from one creation than another, then Lucifer was the one. *"You were in Eden. . . You were anointed as a guardian cherub."* Lucifer was an angel, assigned to guarding the Garden of Eden. *"You were on the holy mount of God."* Lucifer saw Jesus sitting at the right hand of the Father, part of His inner circle perhaps. *"You were blameless in your ways from the day you were created until wickedness was found in you ... and you sinned."* Although Lucifer was created blameless, he later fell into sin. *"So I drove you in disgrace from the mount of God."* There is no room for sin in heaven. *"Your heart became proud on account of your beauty and you corrupted your wisdom because of your splendor. So I threw you to the earth."* The Bible says he took one third of the angels with him, those angels with whom he was conspiring.

Isaiah 14:13 tells us the following: *"You said in your heart, I will ascend to heaven; I will raise my throne above the stars of God. I will sit enthroned on the mount of assembly, on the utmost heights of the sacred mountain. I will ascend above the tops of the clouds, I will make myself like the Most High.*" So what was Lucifer's sin? He wanted to become God. He desired the worship that was for God alone. Don't ever let anyone tell you that one day you can become God. God is a jealous God (Exodus 20:4) and doesn't want any competition.

Satan today stands in opposition to everything God created, everything God intends to accomplish. Jesus said in John 10:10 that He (Jesus) came in order that we might have a full (abundant) life, but the thief comes only to steal and kill and destroy. Satan is at war with God and, unfortunately, we are the collateral damage from his opposition to God.

Paul said in Ephesians 6:12, *"For our struggle is not against flesh and blood, but against the rulers, against the authorities, against the powers of this dark world and against the spiritual forces of evil in the heavenly realms."* There is spiritual warfare going on that we can't see, between the forces of good and evil, between God's angels and Satan's angels.

If there is warfare, there must be an army. Satan is the general of his army. Under him in this army are fallen angels, demons, and humans that have yielded to Satan's control. Although we may not be aware of the battles going on between angels in the heavenly realm, Daniel 10:12-13 made mention of this very fact. An answer to Daniel's prayer was delayed because the angel coming to Daniel's aid had to first fight against the Prince of the Persian kingdom, a supernatural creature who was directing Satan's work in the spirit realm.

While angels operate in the spirit realm, demons operate in the earthly realm. While on earth, Jesus cast out demons, not angels. Demons can harass (influence) people as well as inhabit their bodies. While we may not be aware of battles going on in the heavenly realm, many of us have felt the presence of a demon hindering us while we attempt to obey God's will. The enemy turns up the heat anytime we get on fire for God and start to follow Jesus. If we resist them, the Bible says demons (and Satan) will leave us alone (James 4:7).

Humans can be brought under the control of Satan and used by him to perpetrate evil throughout the world. Drug dealers, gang leaders, serial killers, terrorists, rapists, child abusers, scam artists, and some political leaders fall into this category. You must remember that these people are not the enemy; the enemy is Satan.

Satan is referred to as an accuser of the brothers (Revelation 12:10), a deceiver of nations (Revelation 20:3), a liar and murderer (John 8:44), and a tempter (Matthew 4:3). The Bible says in 1 Peter 5:8, *"Be self-controlled and alert. Your enemy the devil prowls around like a roaring lion looking for someone to devour."* Satan is ruthless and persistent. He tried to have Jesus killed on numerous occasions: by Herod in Matthew 2:13-18, by the townspeople in Luke 4:28-30, by Satan himself in Luke 4:9-10, by the Pharisees in John 8:59, and by the Jews in John 10:31. He wouldn't hesitate to have <u>us</u> killed, except for the protecting power of Jesus.

Although Satan is a formidable enemy, he is not all-powerful, he is not all-knowing (he can't read our minds), and he is not present everywhere like God is. 1 John 4:4b says, *"The one who is in you (God) is greater than the one who is in the world (Satan)."* Praise God.

APPLICATION:

1. Have you ever felt like the path you are on is one leading to your total destruction?
2. Do you know anyone whose life has been, or is being destroyed by Satan?

Memory Verse:

1 Peter 5:8 *"Be self-controlled and alert. Your enemy the devil prowls around like a roaring lion looking for someone to devour."*

Satan Has a Three-Fold Strategy to Destroy Us

Satan would prefer that people worshipped him rather than God, but most people would not willingly choose to follow the devil. So he does the next best thing. As his first line of attack, he gets us to love ourselves rather than God and to exalt ourselves above God. The degree to which a man lives for himself is the degree to which he is filled with the spirit of Satan, says C.S. Lovett in his book <u>Dealing with the Devil</u>.[5] "Look at my accomplishments, look at my success," we cry as we pound our chests. That is why Jesus said we must deny ourselves if we are to follow him (Luke 9:23). Let go of the love of self.

Secondly, Satan tries to seduce us to follow the ways of the world, to feed our appetite for money, power, prestige, popularity, pleasure and success. "It's all about me," is the cry of our subconscious. But James 4:4 says, *"Anyone who chooses to be a friend of the world becomes an enemy of God."* Let go of the love of the world and all that it offers.

Finally, Satan uses distractions (TV, internet, social networks, sports, movies, and entertainment) to make us idle and ineffective for God's kingdom. God is dismayed by believers who sit idly by, while the world is being overtaken by Satan. God is calling us to take a stand in the fight against Satan. We will talk more about that later.

Key Principle: Satan stole from man his authority over the earth.

When God created man, God gave dominion over the earth to man. Subdue it and rule over it are God's commands to Adam in Genesis 1:28. God delegated authority over the earth to man. God placed the earth under Adam's authority and Adam under God's authority. When Adam and Eve sinned against God by eating the forbidden fruit in the Garden of Eden, man placed his authority under Satan, by choosing to obey Satan rather than God.[6] Romans 6:16 says, *"Don't you know that when you offer yourselves to someone to obey him as slaves, you are slaves to the one whom you obey?"* So Satan took over authority over the earth that God had intended for man.

Besides taking authority away from man, Satan also tried to get Jesus to surrender His authority. (Jesus was never under the authority of Satan and He demonstrated this by casting out demons.) Luke 4:5-7 tells the story of Satan tempting Jesus while He was in the wilderness, fasting. *"The devil led him up to a high place and showed him in an instant all the kingdoms of the world. And he said to him, 'I will give you all their <u>authority</u> and splendor, for it has been given to me, and I can give it to anyone I want to. So if you worship me, it will all be yours.'"* Satan was reminding Jesus that he was now in authority on earth and he wanted Jesus under his authority as well.

Jesus didn't rebuke Satan when he said he was in authority. In fact, Jesus later referred to Satan as the "prince of this world" (John 12:31). In 1 John 5:19 we are told, *"The whole world is under the control of the evil one."* So clearly Satan is in authority over the earth, and initially over all who are born on the earth as descendants of Adam. (Note that Jesus did not fall under Satan's authority when He was born on the earth because He did not have an earthly father, being born of a virgin. Since Jesus was conceived by the Holy Spirit, He was not Adam's descendant. He was both fully God and fully man). It was Adam, a man, who surrendered authority to Satan, and Jesus, the man, would take it back for all men. Jesus did this by refusing to surrender his authority to Satan, by living a life without sin, and then dying on the cross, in obedience to God the Father, as a sacrificial offering for all of men's sins. Jesus ultimately defeated Satan when he rose from the dead.

So we can now choose to follow Jesus and be under His authority, and get out from under Satan's authority. However, if we don't choose to be under the authority of Jesus, we are, by birthright, still under the authority of Satan. Jesus said in Luke 11:23, *"He who is not with me is against me."* There is no middle ground. What is your choice? Under whose authority will you reside?

APPLICATION:

1. Is Satan working to make your life ineffective for the kingdom of God? If you're not sure, look at how much time you spend on TV, internet, and entertainment as opposed to reading your Bible, worshipping God, and demonstrating God's love by serving others. Will you do something to increase your effectiveness for God?

2. Which of the world's ways (money, power, prestige, popularity, pleasure, or success) are most enticing to you?

3. What new thing has God revealed to you? Record it in the appendix.

4. Since we are born under Satan's authority, can you see why Jesus said we had to be born again? (John 3:3) He meant that we had to be reborn under the authority of Jesus. Are you ready to be reborn under Jesus' authority? If so, read on.

Memory Verse:

James 4:4b *"Anyone who chooses to be a friend of the world becomes an enemy of God."*

Jesus Conquered Death

Jesus died to take our punishment of death and place it upon Himself. He said in John 3:16-17, *"For God so loved the world that he gave his one and only Son, that whoever believes in him shall not perish but have eternal life. For God did not send his Son into the world to condemn the world, but to save the world through him."* We already learned that our sin (rebellion against God) results in death. Since we are all sinners, we are all doomed to eternal separation from God. But God, out of His great love for us, sent His only Son, to take our punishment of death, so that we don't have to die. Whoever believes that Jesus is the Son of God, that Jesus died on the cross to pay for his sins, and rose again from the dead to conquer death, will be saved to a new life.

Man is not able to get out from under Satan's authority by doing good works. The Bible says it is only by God's grace that we are saved through faith in Jesus Christ, and not through good deeds (Ephesians 2:8-9). It is only by Jesus' death on the cross that Satan's authority is destroyed, that the curse of the "law of sin and death" is broken.

Key Principle: Jesus is the only way to heaven. He has the keys to the kingdom of heaven. Choose Jesus.

Is Jesus really the only way? That's what Jesus Himself said. In John 14:6, Jesus said, *"I am the way and the truth and the life. No one comes to the Father except through me."* In John 3:36, the disciple John said, *"Whoever believes in the Son has eternal life, but whoever rejects the Son will not see life, for God's wrath remains on him."*

Jesus is the only one who provides a way for our sins to be erased, so we can be spared God's judgment against us for our sin. Others may argue, "I'm erasing my sin by doing good deeds." My question to them would be, "How's that working for you? Are you becoming a more loving parent, spouse, neighbor, or friend? Are you developing your relationship with God? Are you able to forgive those who have wronged you? Has God changed your heart? Do you find yourself still sinning?"

Jesus has already paid the penalty for our sin. He has experienced death so that we don't have to. He is inviting us to join in a relationship with Him, to become one of His followers. He longs to be in relationship with us. His death is a gift that He offers freely to everyone. His gift to us is to take away our sin so we can live in Heaven with Him for eternity. But you have to accept the gift. John 1:12 says, *"Yet to all who received him, to those who believed in his name, he gave the right to become children of God."* When you receive the gift, you then become a child of God. You are no longer under Satan's authority.

How do I receive the gift, you may wonder. Pray a prayer like this, "Dear Jesus, I am a sinner and need forgiveness. I ask You to forgive my sins. Thank You for dying on the cross to pay for my sins. I want to change the way I am living my life. I invite You into my heart, to reside there. I invite You to be the leader of my life."

If you prayed a prayer like that, from the heart, the Bible says you are "born again," under the authority of Jesus. *"Therefore, if anyone is in Christ, he is a new creation; the old has gone, the new has come!"* (2 Corinthians 5:17).

Read Luke 15:11-24, the parable of the prodigal son.

A parable is a story with a deeper meaning. Most parables Jesus taught were about God or His kingdom. The parable of the prodigal son shows the love of a father for his son, even after the son has sinned against his father and walked out on him. The son realizes how selfish he has been and returns to the father, asking forgiveness. He wants only to be under his father's roof. The father has been longing for his son to return to him, and when he sees him approaching from a distance, he runs to him. After his son's confession, the father does not rebuke his son; instead he receives him gladly and restores him to full rights of son-ship in the family. Then he celebrates the return of his son.

This parable is about our Heavenly Father. God will take you back if you return to Him in an attitude of repentance, being sorry for your sins and asking for forgiveness. Tell Him you have messed things up and you need His divine help. He will restore you to the title, "child of God" and celebrate your return to the family. He won't be angry with you, but instead will embrace you with joy and rejoicing.

Just before telling this story, Jesus said in Luke 15:10, *"There is rejoicing in the presence of the angels of God over one sinner who repents."* God rejoices with the angels in Heaven when we invite Jesus to take control of our life. Would you like a party in Heaven for you? Come back to your Father.

APPLICATION:

1. The bible says in Romans 10:9, *"That if you confess with your mouth, 'Jesus is Lord,' and believe in your heart that God raised him from the dead, you will be saved."* To confess literally means to agree with, and so therefore, we say so out loud. Do you agree that Jesus is your Lord and Savior? Then pray a prayer similar to the one written above, asking forgiveness for your sins, thanking Jesus for dying for you, and inviting Him to be the Lord of your life. Do you believe God raised Him from the dead and He is alive today? The Bible says He appeared to over 500 witnesses after His resurrection from the dead (1 Corinthians 15:6). If you have both confessed and believed, then you are saved.

2. Jesus warned in Luke 16:13 that *"No servant can serve two masters. Either he will hate the one and love the other, or he will be devoted to the one and despise the other."* Who was your master prior to asking Jesus to be so? Was it a gang leader, money, your corporate boss, materialism, drug dependency, sexual craving, desire for fame? Jesus wants to be your only master, the Lord of your life. Will you stop serving every other master but Jesus?

3. John 1:12 says, *"Yet to all who received him, to those who believed in his name, he gave the right to become children of God."* You are a "child of God" if you prayed the prayer asking Jesus to be the leader of your life. You are no longer under the authority of Satan, but under the authority of Jesus. You are no longer condemned through the "law of sin and death." *"Therefore, there is now no condemnation for those who are in Christ Jesus, because through Christ Jesus the law of the Spirit of life set me free from the law of sin and death"* (Romans 8:1).

Memory Verse:

Romans 10:9 *"That if you confess with your mouth, "Jesus is Lord," and believe in your heart that God raised him from the dead, you will be saved."*

Your Inheritance in the Family of God

You may be thinking, "Now I have to start being good; the fun times are over." Certainly, God does want you to be holy. But just for inviting Jesus into your heart, you get some immediate blessings.

1. You are adopted into His family. The Bible says, in Romans 8:15, we get to call God "Daddy" ("Abba" in Hebrew). He is the perfect dad. He loves unconditionally, encourages us, gives gifts, provides affirmation that we are His, disciplines us in a loving way when we stray, and protects and provides for us. Since we have a formidable enemy in Satan, I am glad I am under the protection of the Most High God.

2. You are forgiven of your sins when you ask. *"If we confess our sins, he is faithful and just and will forgive us our sins and purify us from all unrighteousness"* (1 John 1:9). Having been washed clean of our sins, God views us as righteous individuals. We are now at peace with God. We can come into His holy presence and have a relationship with Him, ask for His help, ask for His blessings, and begin to be changed from the inside out.

3. He begins to restore the years that the locusts have taken

away (Joel 2:25). He will make up for the time that you were lost, rebellious, lonely, downtrodden, or buried in sin. He will begin to restore your life and give you back that lost time.

4. He will remove your heart that has been hardened by sin and replace it with a pliable heart. *"I will give you a new heart and put a new spirit in you; I will remove from you your heart of stone and give you a heart of flesh"* (Ezekiel 36:26). God will begin to soften your heart. He will take away the hurt, resentment, and bitterness, and He will bring healing. He will transplant His own heart into your body, and you will have a heart for the same things the Father does.

5. He will not let anyone snatch you out of His hand (John 10:28). The devil wants to reclaim you as his, but God is there to fight for you. As Satan tries to seduce you to follow the ways of the world, Jesus will encourage you to live a holy and Godly life, and to remain under the authority of Jesus. If Satan is able to draw you away from Jesus, Jesus will fight to return you to His flock.

6. You are instantly part of a royal priesthood (1 Peter 2:9). You become royalty because Jesus is your king and you belong to His household of believers. You become a priest because uniting with Christ grants us entry into God's holy presence to bring Him praise and worship. Like priests, we are also set apart for His use.

7. You automatically come into a new inheritance, which includes eternal life with God in Heaven. In Mathew 25:34, Jesus said, *"Come, you who are blessed by my Father; take your inheritance, the kingdom prepared for you since the creation of the world."*

8. You will reign in life (Romans 5:17) if you consistently walk with Jesus. You will rise to a position of influence among your peers. You will have innovative and creative ideas. Others will scratch their heads trying to figure out why you are so good at what you do. People will seek you out for your advice. Everything you set out to do will be rewarded with successful completion.[7]

9. Your basic needs will be met (Philippians 4:19). As the good provider, God will see to it that your needs are satisfied. You will be fulfilled in so many ways.

Hmmm. Maybe it's worth it to give up that sin I used to enjoy so much in order to partake of promises I never dreamed possible.

APPLICATION:

1. Wow, can all these blessings be mine just for wanting to turn from my sinful ways and conduct my life in a way that is pleasing to Jesus? Yes, if you truly desire to follow after Him. Psalm 84:11 says, *"No good thing does he withhold from those whose walk is blameless."*

2. Which of the above nine blessings most excites you? Why?

3. Occasionally we all break fellowship with God when we sin again. Therefore, we need to know how to restore that fellowship. When God's Spirit speaks to you to tell you that something you just did was not pleasing to Him, agree with Him. Don't make excuses. Ask for His forgiveness. *"If we confess our sins, he is faithful and just and will forgive us our sins and purify us from all unrighteousness"* (1 John 1:9). Then believe that you have been forgiven and thank Him for forgiving you. Trust God to change your wrong attitudes and to change your heart regarding your sin.

4. When we confess our sins, we should no longer feel guilty. *"Then I acknowledged my sin to you and did not cover up my*

iniquity. I said, 'I will confess my transgressions to the Lord'—
and you forgave the guilt of my sin" (Psalm 32:5).

Memory Verse:

2 Corinthians 5:17 *"Therefore, if anyone is in Christ, he is a new*
creation; the old has gone, the new has come!"

Public Acknowledgment

Key Principle: Everything is established in the presence of witnesses. Read Matthew 18:15-20.

In Biblical times, business was conducted at the city gates. Business agreements were made with a handshake, before witnesses. In Matthew 18:15-17, Jesus begins by telling us how to settle a dispute with a Christian brother. Go to the person and try to resolve it one-to-one. If that does not work, bring witnesses to the table who can verify your story, and then try to work it out. He reminds his listeners of the Hebrew law that every matter may be established by the testimony of witnesses.

Jesus then explains that this principle of making agreements before witnesses is a spiritual law as well. As John Bevere explains in Honor's Reward, whatever spoken agreement you reach on earth, between God and yourself, before witnesses, will stand in heaven.[8] If you have chosen to identify with Christ, and to no longer be under Satan's authority, if you will declare it before God and witnesses, it will be established in heaven as well as on earth. Notice in verse 16 it says that it is out of the (spoken) testimony of two, or even three, that words are established. And in verse 18 it says that whatever is bound in the physical realm will be bound in the spiritual realm as well. That is one reason why Jesus said to be baptized. Baptism is a public testimony of your faith in front of witnesses. That is why the Bible says in Psalm 107:2, *"Let the redeemed of the Lord say this."* That is why you are supposed to tell someone when you pray the prayer of salvation, inviting Jesus to be the Lord and master of your life. That is why the Bible says to share your testimony of what God has done for you (1 Peter 3:15). By doing so, by publicly declaring so, you are establishing before witnesses that you are under the authority of Jesus Christ, and that Satan no longer has any authority over you. Satan and his entire realm of followers will know that they have no claim on you. You are now marked with the seal of the Holy Spirit. There is now no question whose authority is over you. Revelation 12:11 says, when speaking about the brothers who make up the kingdom of God, *"They overcame him (Satan) by the blood of the Lamb and by the word of their testimony."*

In verses 19-20, Jesus extends this principle to prayer. If you come before God with witnesses, and are in agreement about what you are asking, your prayer will be answered. This is the most powerful method of lifting up prayer requests to God, to ask publicly, before God and witnesses who are in agreement, what you desire.

APPLICATION:

1. Have you been baptized? Have you given a testimony of how you came to faith? These are examples of how your salvation is established in both the earthly realm and the spiritual realm. Will you commit to a public acknowledgement of your faith?

2. Have you ever prayed out loud with another believer, being in agreement with that person, and asking in faith for God to do something big in your life for God's kingdom?

3. Can you share your testimony if you are asked? Try writing it down, using the appendix.

Memory Verse:

Luke 12:8 *"I tell you, whoever acknowledges me before men, the Son of Man will also acknowledge him before the angels of God."*

The Fruitful Life

Key Principle: The evidence of a redeemed life is seen in the fruit it produces.
Read Matthew 13: 3-23, the parable of the sower.

In this story, a farmer sows (scatters) seed on the ground for planting. Some falls on a path and is eaten by birds. Some seed falls on rocky soil, but the roots are too shallow for the plants to survive. Other seed falls among weeds and gets choked out. But some seed falls among fertile soil and produces the intended crop. Jesus goes on to explain the parable. The seed is the word of God, the message of salvation. The farmer is God, who is spreading His word wherever He chooses. And the soil is the heart of man. What happens when the seed is planted in a person's heart? There are four possible outcomes. The first is that the person will reject the message. Because the message of salvation is rejected, there is no way for the seed to take root. The second possibility is that the person will stop seeking Jesus when persecuted by his friends. They might mock, "What, are you a Christian now?" The seed was beginning to grow, but before it had a chance to take root, was scorched by the sun. The third possibility is that the person will become too busy to have time for God. This person may believe for a while, but then becomes more interested in pursuing the ways of the world than in seeking to know God. The weeds of life choke off the growth. The final possibility is that the person will hear the message of salvation, accept it with all his heart, and join in a relationship with Jesus and other believers where the seed can receive plenty of sun, water, and nutrients. This person receives the word of God and acts on it. The seed develops into a thriving plant and produces an abundant harvest of food, represented by thriving Christ-like relationships, investing time and money in the kingdom of God, and telling others about Christ. According to the parable, the seed has the potential to multiply 100-fold.

The meaning of this parable was not lost on Jesus' audience. Farmers knew the only productive outcome was the last one, producing a bountiful harvest. And so it is with God. He desires that all believers continually live lives of fruitful obedience to Him.

Jesus teaches something else in this passage. In Matthew 13:10, the disciples asked Jesus why he spoke in parables. Jesus explained that it was so those who had calloused hearts would not be able to understand the message. He only wanted those who were truly seeking the truth to find the answers for which they were searching.

APPLICATION:

This parable is one of the few that Jesus explained in depth. He really wants us to understand that those who reject the message of salvation or those who receive it but later put their faith on a shelf in order to avoid persecution or to pursue the pleasures of the world, that these people are not standing firm to the end. We need to stand resolved to not let the siren call of the world pull us away from following Him. Will you continue planting seeds among your friends, family members, and associates who may have rejected Jesus or turned from following Him and pray for God to bring the seed to full maturity?

Memory Verse:

Matthew 24:13 *"But he who stands firm to the end will be saved."*

Week 3

God Wants a Relationship with You

Key Principle: Eternal life is all about having a relationship with God.

If you have decided to be a follower of Jesus, the goal is to then have a personal relationship with God and with Jesus. In John 17:3, Jesus said, *"Now this is eternal life: that they may <u>know</u> you, the only true God, and Jesus Christ, whom you have sent."* In the Greek translation, the word "know" meant to have a relationship on an intimate and personal level. If you want to spend eternity in Heaven, in the presence of your Creator, then the requirement is to have theis personal, intimate relationship with God and with Jesus, while on earth. The best way to do that is to spend time in conversation with God and in His word, meditating on what God is telling you. Then act on it.

To know God fully is to comprehend the depth to which God loves us. He rescued us from a death sentence in Hell through the most incredible way imaginable, by condemning His own Son to a horrible death. His Son is perfect. We are sinners, repulsive to God. Yet He chose to give us the same worth as His own son.

God is an artist who composes incredible beauty. He is a wildly imaginative creator, a wise counselor, a loving father who loves unconditionally, disciplines lovingly, and loves to give gifts to His children. Spend time with Him. Keep a journal of the things He is showing you and revealing to you. Nothing can separate you from His love.

Read Luke 14:16-24, the parable of the great banquet.

A man prepared a great banquet and invited many guests. The guests all began making excuses: I have to attend to the field I just bought, I have to try out my new oxen, I just got married. The host became angry and withdrew his invitation. Instead he invited the poor and downtrodden to his banquet. After that, there was still some room at the table so the host said to go out and search near and far for any that might accept the invitation.

So what is the meaning of this parable? Jesus is preparing the wedding supper of the lamb, a feast prepared to welcome new believers into Heaven (Revelation 19:9). He is inviting us into a relationship with Him, but we often are too indifferent to take the time to get to know Him. We are consumed by work, materialism, and life's happenings. Determined to have every seat occupied at His banquet, Jesus may even give us repeated invitations, but ultimately, if we do not respond, the invitation to know Him will be offered to someone else. We will not have the opportunity to join in the heavenly banquet. Instead, when we die and stand before God, He will say, *"I never knew you."* (Matthew 7:22-23)

Many people are not making the time to know God and His ways because they are busy engaging in what the world has to offer. It is only by having a relationship with God and Jesus that we can be changed in the heart. Only then can we become the people that God wants us to become.

APPLICATION:

1. What would God say about your level of effort to get to know Him personally?

Memory Verse:

John 15:5 *"I am the vine; you are the branches. If a man remains in me and I in him, he will bear much fruit; apart from me you can do nothing."*

God's Promises

The Bible is full of promises that are gifts from God. His promises are given to us to enable us to live a rich and fulfilled life, full of hope and confidence in our Savior. God desires us to be full of prosperity so we can bless others. His promises encourage us to live pure lives, and they help us escape the corrupting influence of sin. Listen to some of these promises.

Acts 16:31b *"Believe in the Lord Jesus, and you will be saved—you and your household."*

Proverbs 8:35 *"For whoever finds me finds life and receives favor from the Lord."*

Psalm 37: 4 *"Delight yourself in the Lord and he will give you the desires of your heart."*

Proverbs 16: 3 *"Commit to the Lord whatever you do, and your plans will succeed."*

Proverbs 16:7 *"When a man's ways are pleasing to the Lord, he makes even his enemies live at peace with him."*

Proverbs 11:25 *"A generous man will prosper; he who refreshes others will himself be refreshed."*

Luke 6:38 *"Give, and it will be given to you. A good measure, pressed down, shaken together and running over, will be poured into your lap. For with the measure you use, it will be measured to you."*

John 15:5 *"I am the vine; you are the branches. If a man remains in me and I in him, he will bear much fruit; apart from me you can do nothing."*

Psalm 55:22 *"Cast your cares on the Lord and he will sustain you; he will never let the righteous fall."*

Psalm 34:7 *"The angel of the Lord encamps around those who fear him, and he delivers them."*

Psalm 33:18-19 *"But the eyes of the Lord are on those who fear him, on those whose hope is in his unfailing love, to deliver them from death and keep them alive in famine."*

Psalm 37:28 *"For the Lord loves the just and will not forsake his faithful ones. They will be protected forever, but the offspring of the wicked will be cut off."*

1 John 1:9 *"If we confess our sins, he is faithful and just and will forgive us our sins and purify us from all unrighteousness."*

1 Peter 3:12 *"For the eyes of the Lord are on the righteous and his ears are attentive to their prayer, but the face of the Lord is against those who do evil."*

Isaiah 56:6b-7 *"All who keep the Sabbath without desecrating it and who hold fast to my covenant—these I will bring to my holy mountain and give them joy in my house of prayer."*

James 1:5 *"If any of you lacks wisdom, he should ask God, who gives generously to all without finding fault, and it will be given to him."*

Exodus 20:12 *"Honor your father and your mother, so that you may live long in the land the Lord your God is giving you."*

Psalm 34:12 *"Whoever of you loves life and desires to see many good days, keep your tongue from evil and your lips from speaking lies."*

Proverbs 3:5-6 *"Trust in the Lord with all your heart and lean not on your own understanding; in all your ways acknowledge him, and he will make your paths straight."*

So why isn't every Christian experiencing all these promises? Listen, a man could be starving to death while standing in an apple orchard with ripe fruit all around him. He has to pick the fruit. Likewise, you have to identify the promise(s) you want to receive from God and establish that this promise is what you are trusting will happen.

How to Cement These Promises into Your Life

First of all, you have to believe that these promises are true. Numbers 23:19 says the following about promises: *"God is not a man, that he should lie, nor a son of man, that he should change his mind. Does he speak and then not act? Does he promise and not fulfill?"* God cannot lie. His word is truth. He will honor his promise to you if you believe.

Secondly, you have to fulfill your part of the promise. Promises are conditional on our obedience to them. There is God's part and there is our part. You have to fulfill your part first in order to receive God's part. If the condition is not met, the promise is negated, not because of God's unfaithfulness but because of our disobedience or lack of faith.

Next, the promise has to be made contractually. Some say believe it, some say claim it, some say speak it. We already learned from

Matthew 18:19 that if you come before God <u>with witnesses</u> and are in agreement for what you are asking, you are establishing a contract between you and God.

Finally, from time to time, restate your covenant with God and review whether you are still fulfilling your part of the agreement.

APPLICATION:

1. Review each of the promises listed above. What is your part in each of them? Circle the condition you must meet.
2. What is God's part in each of the above promises? Underline it.
3. By way of example, if you have a child who has always been respectful of his parents, never been rebellious through his teen years, and brought honor to you by working hard in school to get good grades, then you may want to believe Exodus 20:12 for him/her. Pray over your child, with witnesses present, declaring that your child has always honored his parents. Through faith, declare that you are believing God's promise for your child of a long life. Thank God for His promise and praise His faithfulness. Go forward, believing that the promise is established both in heaven and on earth.

    Let's say you are praying for your dear Aunt Alice to be saved. Your prayer, together with another believer, could go like this: Father God, your word says in Acts 16:31, *"Believe in the Lord Jesus and you will be saved, you and your household."* I believe your promise is true, because You, God, cannot lie. Aunt Alice is a member of my household so I am believing this promise for her salvation. You know I believe in You, in your word, in your redeeming power, and in your ability to make all things happen. Now I stand boldly before your throne asking You to transform her heart to bring her to You. I don't know how You will do this, but I trust that You will, and I am ready to be used in your plan to redeem her life. I believe that You will do what you said You will do. In the name of Jesus. Amen.

Let's say you have a child who was a believer but has wandered away from God. Your prayer might go like this: Father God, your word says in John 10:28-29 that no one can snatch them out of your hand. I believe your word is truth. I am believing this promise for my child and that the good shepherd will go out and find the lost sheep and return him/her to the flock. I trust in You Father and pray for your word to be carried out in my child's life. In the name of Jesus, Amen.

4. For which promises do you want to make a covenant with God? Pray over those verses with your spiritual partner, claiming those promises before witnesses. Record your covenant(s) in the appendix of this book.

5. Some people may tell you that you can't presume to call on God to make a promise with you. They probably don't know about the story in Genesis 32 where Jacob actually wrestled with God until He would give His blessing. They are probably like the man standing in the middle of an orchard full of ripe fruit, but who is starving to death because he hasn't picked any fruit. Don't starve for blessings while God's orchard is full of promises waiting to be claimed.

6. Psalm 145:13 says, *"The Lord is faithful to all his promises."* But will you be?

7. What have you learned that is new? Record it in the appendix.

Memory Verse:

Numbers 23:19 *"God is not a man, that he should lie, nor a son of man, that he should change his mind. Does he speak and then not act? Does he promise and not fulfill?"*

Putting God First

Key Principle: God wants you to love Him above everything else.

Mark 12:30 says, *"Love the Lord your God with all your heart and with all your soul and with all your mind and with all your strength."* God desires that you love Him more than you love yourself, more than you love your hobbies, more than you love your spouse and children and parents and siblings. God wants to be your number one passion in life, your first love. Anything you give your devotion to, over and above God, is an idol. The Bible says that God is a jealous God (Exodus 20:4). If He finds you giving your devotion to something or someone else, He will deal with you about it.

You can demonstrate your love for God by worshipping Him. Revelation 7:9-11 paints a picture of what worship in heaven looks like. People from every nation, tribe, language, and dialect are standing together before the throne of God, crying out praises in unison. God desires that we worship Him with all our heart. God rebuked the nation of Israel in Isaiah 29:13 when he said, *"These people come near to me with their mouth and honor me with their lips, but their hearts are far from me."* Your worship should come from the heart.

You can honor God by giving Him praise in church, by giving an offering of money, by showing up to church on time, by reading the scripture passage, by not falling asleep in church, and by taking notes on the sermon and later meditating on what God wants you to do with that information.

Putting God Ahead of Ourselves

The world teaches us to worship ourselves. If we are to place God first in our lives, we must learn to deny self. Mark 8:34b says, *"If anyone would come after me, he must deny himself and take up his cross and follow me."* Denying self means foregoing my agenda for God's agenda, not being so selfish with my time that I have no time for serving God. Denying self means seeking to glorify God rather than to glorify myself, surrendering my pride and desire for recognition in order that God can be the one who is glorified. Taking up my cross means showing publicly that I belong to Jesus. When the Romans crucified someone for breaking Roman law, the person being killed had to carry his own cross as a sign of submission to Rome. Jesus is asking us to take up our cross publicly as a sign of submission to Him. Following Him is about surrendering to His will for my life and putting into practice the love that Christ showed for others.

APPLICATION:

1. Ask God to give you His heart, to love what He loves and hate what He hates. God hates when we are proud. He hates injustice. God loves when we show others mercy and take care of the oppressed. Try writing a love letter to God. Let Him know what you are thankful for. Tell God why you love Him.
2. We have to surrender daily to God. Pray a prayer like this at the start of every morning: "God, fill me with your Holy Spirit today so that I am not full of myself."

Memory Verse:

Mark 8:34b *"If anyone would come after me, he must deny himself and take up his cross and follow me."*

Satan Wants to Defeat You

If you are not a believer, Satan wants to make sure you do not become one. 2 Corinthians 4:4 says, *"The god of this age has blinded the minds of unbelievers, so that they cannot see the light of the gospel of the glory of Christ, who is the image of God."* Satan has created a world system that excludes God and he wants to draw you into it. 1 John 2:15 tells us this system is all about cravings of the flesh (materialism, control, power), lust of the eyes (sexual immorality, greed), and the boasting of what man has and does (pride and vanity).

If you are a new believer, Satan wants you to quickly lose your newly found joy. Mark 4:15b says, *"As soon as they hear it, Satan comes and takes away the word that was sown in them."* Jesus was describing Satan's desperate attempts to keep the message of the gospel from taking root in new believers' lives.

If you are a rooted believer, Satan wants to neutralize you. 1 Peter 5:8 says, *"Be self-controlled and alert. Your enemy the devil prowls around like a roaring lion looking for someone to devour."* He wants to totally defeat you so that you have no testimony and are not productive for God's kingdom.

If you have not experienced Satan's opposition, then it is probably because you are not a threat to him. But once you make a decision to follow Jesus, or decide to surrender some sin to which you have been clinging, or decide to come alive and live passionately for Christ, you can expect to encounter Satan's resistance during your transition.

Satan's Gateways into Your Life

There are gateways the devil uses to get a foothold in your life, in order to try to take back his authority over you. Be alert so that you do not give Satan an opening, lest he be quick to take advantage.

1. Unforgiveness
Read Matthew 18:23-35, the parable of the unforgiving servant.

In this story, a man who owes a large sum of money is forgiven his debt by his master, but then goes out and demands payment from someone who owes him money. When the master finds out, he takes back his forgiveness of the man's debt and instead, has him thrown into jail and tortured until he pays the master what is owed. The point of the story is this: we have all been forgiven a huge debt, the sin we have committed against our Master. As forgiven people, our only recourse is to forgive others who have wronged us. This is one of the hallmarks of the Christian faith. Further, verse 35 says, *"This is how my heavenly Father will treat each of you unless you forgive your brother from your heart."* This verse implies that if you hold unforgiveness in your heart, instead of being forgiven of your sin, you will receive the same punishment as the man in the parable. Matthew 6:15 says, *"But if you do not forgive men their sins, your Father will not forgive your sins."* Unforgiveness not only results in bitterness, but it opens us to Satan's control over our lives. In 2 Corinthians 2:10-11, the apostle Paul says, *"And what I have forgiven . . . I have forgiven in the sight of Christ for your sake, in order that Satan might not outwit us. For we are not unaware of his schemes."*

2. Holding on to Unconfessed Sin
If you are holding on to some sin that you enjoy, you are

opening yourself up to Satan's re-entry into your life. You are not fully surrendered. To confess literally means to agree with God. We must admit our condition to God in order for Him to help us.

1 John 1:9 says, *"If we confess our sins, he is faithful and just and will forgive us our sins and purify us from all unrighteousness."* Confess your sin to your spiritual partner and ask him/her to pray with you in asking God to help you let go of it.

3. **Rebelliousness**

God has placed authority figures in our lives. He has established authority because He is a God of order. **Read Romans 13:1-5.**

This passage tells us that everyone must submit to the governing authorities placed over us. This authority is established by God, and he who rebels against this authority is rebelling against God. There are numerous authority figures in your life: parents, police, teachers, pastor, elders, even the president of the country. If you do not submit, you harbor the spirit of rebellion and you are giving Satan a foothold to destroy your life. Notice I did not say that Satan makes us rebellious. Rebelliousness comes from wanting to be in control. In order to give up rebellion, one must surrender control to Jesus. Some think it is cool to flaunt their rebellious nature in the way they look or dress, in words and pictures printed on their t-shirts, in the way they drive, or in their attitude toward authority. When they do this, they are painting a bull's eye on their back for Satan to target.

Peter, one of the original twelve disciples of Christ said, in 2 Peter 2:9-10, *"The Lord knows how to rescue godly men from trials and to hold the unrighteous for the day of judgment . . . This is especially true of those who follow the corrupt desire of the sinful nature and despise authority."*

4. **Involvement in the Occult**

The occult includes witchcraft, astrology, fortune telling,

horoscopes, attempting to communicate with the dead, and attempting to know the future so that one can gain an advantage over others. The results of occultism are often dramatic and fascinating, and it is this fascination that draws people into occult practices in the way a prostitute would entice a young man into immorality. The motivation behind the occult is a quest for power or obtaining knowledge supernaturally.[9] These are all ways of invoking Satan's powers and the Bible says to avoid them. Leviticus 19:26 say, *"Do not practice divination or sorcery."*

5. **Activity Leading to Addiction**

When someone is addicted, you know what results. That person will steal and destroy everyone in their path in order to feed their addiction. The addiction often leads to rebellion, hopelessness, violent behavior, or suicide. Satan loves using alcohol and drugs to gain control of a person. He will initially seek to subject the person to intense cravings, then seek to alter the victim's behavior and thought patterns.[10] No recreational user ever sets out to become addicted, but by giving Satan a foothold, he lets him in to destroy his life. The apostle Paul said in 1 Corinthians 6:12b, *"Everything is permissible for me—but I will not be mastered by anything."* Stay away from all that is illegal and use everything else in moderation, or abstain altogether.

6. **Idol Worship**

While you do not often see statues of other gods today, people nevertheless have idols in their lives. Their devotion goes to cars, homes, clothes, their 401K, their bodies, boats, motorcycles, vacation homes, etc. It has been said that a person can tell where one's devotion lies by looking at his checkbook to see where his money is being spent. Exodus 20:4-6 tells us we shall not worship idols.

Others believe that inanimate objects hold some kind of spiritual power. They have them around the house or on their person. Some tattoo satanic symbols on their arms and claim extra strength. All of these anger God and result in His protection being removed.

7. Marrying Outside the Faith.

This happened to Solomon, the third king of Israel. He adopted the religious customs of his many wives and forgot his own faith, resulting in falling out of favor with God. There are many examples of this today. Someone marries a person of another religion or a person with no religion and then abandons his own faith. The command, *"Do not be yoked together with unbelievers"* (2 Corinthians 6:14), applies not only to spouses, but also business partners, lenders, counselors, doctors, etc.

8. Gossip, Slander, and Judgment of Others

James 1:26 says, *"If anyone considers himself religious and yet does not keep a tight rein on his tongue, he deceives himself and his religion is worthless."* Ouch! Jesus said in Matthew 12:36, *"But I tell you that men will have to give account on the day of judgment for every careless word they have spoken."* Double ouch!! Proverbs 18:21 says, *"The tongue has the power of life and death."* We can speak praises and blessings into peoples' lives (the power of life) or we can speak curses over them (the power of death). Don't ever tell people they are worthless or won't amount to anything; instead tell them they can achieve greatness.

Some of the most common curses that come out of our mouths are curses on us. "I'll never get promoted at this company," "I'll never get well," and "This pressure is killing me" can all become self-fulfilling prophesies when you speak a curse over yourself. Don't invite a controlling spirit into your life with idle words. Let the words of David, written in Psalm 141:3, be your prayer. *"Set a guard over my mouth, O Lord; keep watch over the door of my lips."*

9. **Going It Alone**

In 1 Peter 5:8, Satan is compared to a lion stalking his prey, looking for someone to devour. So then, if you want to defend yourself against Satan, do what animals do in the wild to defend against lions. They stay in herds and rely on one another for safety. Likewise, you should not attempt to go it alone in your journey with Jesus. Some suggestions are to attend a weekly Bible study at your church, to be in a small group that meets weekly in someone's home, or to meet regularly with a spiritual partner with whom you can share your struggles and pray for one another. These activities will introduce you to other Christians. You can gain strength from the struggles and victories that other Christians are experiencing. God calls us to be in community with other believers, not only for our own growth but so we can build up others, encourage them, and pray for them. When a believer falls, he/she needs to have a spiritual partner to help him/her up.

10. **Hanging with the Wrong People**

1 Corinthians 15:33 says, *"Do not be misled: Bad company corrupts good character."* Some people will never mature spiritually unless they get free from the people who are corrupting them. Ask God for new friends. He will supply them.

APPLICATION:

1. Now that you are knowledgeable about spiritual warfare and the tactics of the enemy, you do not have to be afraid of Satan, but you do have to keep up your guard. You can look around you and probably see someone you know who has fallen under the control of Satan, or wandered from their faith. God's word has forewarned us of the enemy's tactics so we can be victorious. Please do not take these warnings lightly.

2. Know that pastors, elders, deacons, teachers, and others in authority in the church are fully in Satan's sights. If Satan can

bring one of them down, he can sometimes destroy an entire church. Will you pray for your spiritual leaders?

3. From the above list of 10 gateways Satan uses to get a foothold in your life, what are the ones he is most likely to use against you?

    What is God telling you to do about it? Make note of this in the appendix.

4. Are there any gateways that Satan is already using against you to gain a foothold in your life? If you are serious about keeping Satan from controlling you, will you honestly admit those gateways, confess them before God, and ask your prayer partner to pray with you for deliverance?

Memory Verse:

Ephesians 6:12 *"For our struggle is not against flesh and blood, but against the rulers, against the authorities, against the powers of this dark world and against the spiritual forces of evil in the heavenly realms."*

Opposing Satan

The author C. S. Lovett, in his book <u>Dealing with the Devil</u>, teaches that there are two specific tactics for dealing with the enemy. One is used before Satan shows up, and the other is used when he is present. 2 Corinthians 10:4 says, *"The weapons we fight with are not the weapons of the world. On the contrary, they have divine power to demolish strongholds."*

Before Satan Shows Up, Watch and Pray[11]

In Matthew 26:41, Jesus told his disciples, *"Watch and pray so that you will not fall into temptation."*

<u>Watch</u> for the ways Satan is most likely to attack you. You know the areas where you are vulnerable. If you struggle with alcohol, do not take a drink. If you struggle with pornography, do not open the Victoria Secret catalogue when it appears in your mailbox. If aggressive drivers set you off, get out of the fast lane and let them pass.

Then <u>pray</u> that you do not fall into temptation. Pray for God's "hedge of protection" (from Job 1:10) to be placed around you. If Satan tried to have Jesus killed, do you think he would hesitate to destroy you?

After Satan Shows Up, Confront
Read Ephesians 6:13-18

This passage lists weapons that God gives us in our fight against Satan. Most are defensive weapons, but there is one offensive weapon, the sword of the Spirit. Verse seventeen says the sword is the word of God. When Satan attacks, do what Jesus did. First quote scripture, then, declare out loud, "In the name of Jesus, be gone." The Bible says we are to resist Satan. This is not the time to pray, but the time to confront. You have all the tools you need to do it on your own.

For example, let's say you are spending time worrying about something you cannot control. This might be how you confront, saying it out loud: "The Bible says, 'Cast all your cares on the Lord, and he will sustain you.' I have done that and now I am trusting in God to take care of me. Satan be gone from me in the name of Jesus."

Generational Curses

Some sins can be found in the same family for several generations. Look to your siblings, your parents, your grandparents, or your great grandparents. Are there any patterns of sin that run throughout your family history? Sexual immorality, extramarital affairs, child abuse, drug addiction, greed, disregard for authority, idol worship, anger, or even voodoo? Now look at how those same relatives are coping with life. Is there a pattern of failed relationships, divorce, chronic poor health, poverty, failure, or even suicide? Your family may be under a generational curse. You are going to have to be especially watchful that you do not fall into sin in those areas while petitioning God to break the curse that may eventually come upon you. Even if a particular sin is not passed down to the next generation, the curse may still be passed along if the children are estranged from God. An example of this is found in Exodus 20:5 where God is forbidding idol worship. *"You shall not bow down to them or worship them; for I, the Lord your God, am a jealous God, punishing the children for the sin of the fathers to the third and fourth generation of those who hate me, but showing love to a thousand generations of those who love me and keep my commandments."* Do you want to bless your children? Keep God's commandments and love God. But continue in a pattern of disobedience and disdain for God, and you may bring disaster upon your children.

To break the curse, examine what sin caused it, confess it, and ask forgiveness. Renounce the curse by declaring that Jesus' death on the cross overcame the curse and claim the promise of Galatians 3:13, *"Christ redeemed us from the curse of the law by becoming a curse for us."* Confront Satan by stating out loud, "I am a child of the most high God and I am redeemed by the blood of Jesus. Satan, be gone from me and take your curse with you."

APPLICATION:

1. Watch! In what area is Satan most likely to attack you? Is it lust, being judgmental, gossip, lack of faith, laziness, worrying, coveting? Be on your guard and be praying for God's hedge of protection in these areas. Pray the devil does not tempt you or, if he does, that you will have the courage to stand. 1 Corinthians 10:13 says, *"No temptation has seized you except what is common to man. And God is faithful; he will not let you be tempted beyond what you can bear. But when you are tempted, he will also provide a way out so that you can stand up under it."*

2. When you feel like things are crumbling all around you, it may be that you are under attack from Satan. After all, pain, suffering, disease, sickness, strife, worry, coveting, and relational conflict were never part of God's plan for creation. Remind Satan that Jesus conquered these things on the cross. "By His stripes I am healed. Jesus has overcome the world." Tell Satan, "I am a child of the most high God and, in the name of Jesus, Satan, be gone." Satan may not fear you but he does fear Jesus. You must say it out loud since nowhere in the Bible does it say Satan can read minds. Say it with authority because you are now under the authority of Jesus Christ. James 4:7 says, *"Resist the devil and he will flee from you."*

3. Satan is also known as an accuser of the brothers. If you feel

like he is accusing you or laying a guilt trap for you, rebuke him. It is the Holy Spirit who convicts us of our sin and when we confess it and ask forgiveness, it is forgiven. Jesus paid it all on the cross. Satan has no business accusing us or making us feel guilty. Isaiah 54:17 says, *"No weapon formed against you will prevail and you will refute every tongue that accuses you."*

4. Listen, you have spiritual authority over demons. They will have no place in your life if you are fully yielded to God, that is, not secretly holding onto some un-confessed sin, not denying someone forgiveness, not loving things of this world more than God, etc.

5. What new things did you learn? Write them down in the appendix.

Memory Verse:

James 4:7b *"Resist the devil and he will flee from you."*

Focused on Eternity

Key Principle: Your choices in this life determine your future in the next life.

Your life on this earth is a test, as Rick Warren said in his book, <u>The Purpose Driven Life</u>. [12] The first and most important test is "What did you do with Jesus?" If you accepted that His death on the cross was in payment for your sin, you chose to pursue Him, you worshiped Him from your heart, and spent time getting to know Him, then you get to go to Heaven, to enjoy a relationship with Him, and worship Him in person. Likewise, if you had no desire to pursue a relationship with Him while on earth, then you will not be invited to spend eternity with Him after you die.

The second test is "What did you do during your time on earth to serve Him?" Jesus said in Luke 12:48b, *"From everyone who has been given much, much will be demanded."* We all have been given much, the greatest gifts anyone could get: forgiveness of our sins and eternal life. You should be all about understanding what it is God wants you to do with your life in order to serve Him, and then get on with doing it.

You will continue to be tested all along the way. God will test your character; He will test your resolve to stay connected to Jesus; He will test to see if you are a good steward of the resources with which He has blessed you; and He will test your faithfulness. To those who pass the tests, there will be great reward and great joy.

Eternal Perspective

Depending on what goals you have for yourself, high school can look very different for many people. If you have no goals, you may decide high school is a waste of time and drop out as soon as the law allows. If your goal is to work immediately after high school, you may have a goal to take a class in business, or electronics, or keyboarding, or database management. You may be aiming to attend a vocational school after high school to learn a trade. If your goal is to go to college, then classes in math, science, and the humanities will be important to you. You should certainly live your life with your intermediate goals in focus. Likewise, you should live your life with your ultimate destiny in focus.

If you have no plans for the afterlife, then you might live this life with one goal in mind, to get all you can get out of this life. Your focus may be to accumulate wealth for a comfortable life on earth, to always have the finest things money can buy, to have a beautiful wife, even if it means trading up for a prettier one every 10 years. Maybe your goal is to attain a lofty status in your professional field or to achieve fame and influence among your peers. Maybe you want to be very popular and to fit into the world's social order.

But if you have a goal to live in Heaven for all eternity, your focus will be very different. Acquiring a lot of stuff will no longer be so important; after all, you can not take it with you and you are only here for a relatively short time. Living comfortably may become less important than developing a compassion for the poor, downtrodden, and oppressed. Obtaining God's approval will become more important than obtaining the world's approval. Developing your character will be more important than achieving status. Learning to love people will be more important than always coming out on top competitively. Learning to share will be more important than accumulating stuff. Learning to be compassionate will be more important than always being right. Teaching people about Jesus will be more important than teaching them how to become successful. There are plenty of resources to tell us how to succeed in this life. We need to make sure our focus is on preparation for the next life.

The Bible warns us not to get caught up in the ways of the world: pursuing earthly success, self-promotion, and personal accomplishment. The apostle Paul said, in Colossians 3:2, *"Set your minds on things above, not on earthly things."* The disciple Peter advised, in 1 Peter 2:ll, that we should be *"aliens and strangers in the world."* We must die to pursuing the things of this world and live to keeping our focus on eternity.

APPLICATION:
Read Luke 10:38-42.

1. Your relationship with God is the most important thing. To spend time serving God, at the expense of developing your relationship with God, is the wrong choice. What lifestyle change do you have to make in order to make time for your relationship with God and to have the proper balance between serving and abiding in God's presence?

2. The Bible says in Galatians 6:2, *"Carry each other's burdens, and in this way you will fulfill the law of Christ."* What lifestyle change do you have to make in order to care for the hurting people God has placed in your path and to have money available to help those in need?

3. How can you learn to care less about your own welfare and be more concerned about others?

4. Since we cannot take it (money, possessions) with us, we are wise to invest in the work of God's kingdom, rather than investing in something that is temporal. What kind of vain goals are you pursuing? Here are some examples: traveling to every continent, becoming the president of a company, buying your dream house, having the best of everything money can buy, having kids who excel in sports, looking like you are in your thirties when you are in your fifties, driving luxury cars, living in a large house.

5. What kind of eternal goals are you pursuing? For example:

supporting a missionary couple to advance the gospel over-
seas, constructing homes and wells in poor regions of the
world, teaching the gospel to the youth of your church, helping to rebuild homes and lives of people caught in natural
disasters, funding an education for an orphan, weekly visit-
ing a jail or nursing home in your community, leaving your
church home to support a church plant in another community, hosting a Bible study in your home, serving on Sunday
morning in your church, becoming a missionary yourself.

Memory Verse:

Colossians 3:2 *"Set your minds on things above, not on earthly
things."*

Week 4

Knowing God's Will for My Life

You will only discover God's will for your life when you are willing to take the first step in whatever direction He leads. As you read His word, listen to a sermon, read a book on a spiritual topic, talk to other believers about their ministries and experiences, or spend time communicating with God, always ponder where it is that God is leading you. Close your mind to any negative thoughts like, "I could never do that," or "That could never happen in my life." Instead, let your enthusiasm be stoked by imagining God working in a mighty way through your life. Be praying that God will show you His next step for your life and then be listening for His answer. If you are asking God to reveal His will and three days later someone invites you to go on a missions trip, be discerning of the fact that God speaks to you through other believers. If you are praying that God shows you how to serve others and several days later you hear about an opportunity to aid the poor in Central America, be aware that God just answered your prayer. If you are invited by another believer to engage in some ministry, say yes, rather than make excuses.

God's plan for your life is an intricate mosaic of many experiences all pieced together. You will seldom see the end goal in the beginning, but only the next step in His plan. God may first bring you to a particular church. Then he may work on your heart to lead you to serve in ministry. Next, someone may invite you to participate in a youth ministry at that church. Meanwhile, God plants a seed in you to attend a class to learn how to share the gospel. God may then give you the opportunity to begin sharing the gospel with the youth you are serving and develop in you a passion for reaching the lost. Along the way, someone may invite you to accompany him as he visits a juvenile lock-up. God may give you a heart for reaching unsaved youth in a part of your city where crime is rampant and parental guidance is lacking. You join in that ministry and experience God using you to reach many unsaved youth and helping to turn around their lives. God next gives you a passion for mentoring some of these youth and giving guidance and meaning to their lives. After awhile, God may have you start a mentoring ministry where you train others how to do what you have learned to do. Then you begin to reproduce yourself by encouraging others to be mentors and sharing your mentoring experiences with them.

It all starts when you ask God to show you the next step for your life, then His plan continues to unfold as you are obedient to act upon it. In Matthew 7:21, Jesus said, *"Not everyone who says to me, 'Lord, Lord,' will enter the kingdom of heaven, but only he who does the will of my Father who is in heaven."* God designed a plan for each of our lives while we were still in the womb (Psalm 139:16). If we are open to discovering that plan and obedient to following God's leading, we will reap great reward when we enter God's kingdom. Ephesians 5:17 says, *"Therefore do not be foolish, but understand what the Lord's will is."* In the beginning of this book, we learned that the degree to which you dig deeply into the word and believe what it says determines the degree to which God opens it up to you. In the same way, the degree to which you seek to know God's will for your life and are obedient to it determines the degree to which God reveals it to you.

APPLICATION:

1. You can not fulfill God's plan for your life while continually focusing on your own plan for your life. List in the appendix one or two areas you feel God is inviting you to explore.

2. In their book, <u>Hearing God's Voice</u>, Henry and Richard Blackaby list dozens of ways that God speaks to us.[13] The most common are these: through reading His word, through authors of books on spiritual topics, through other believers (pastor, church members, Bible study members), and through prayer. What steps are you taking to ensure you are hearing His voice spoken in your own life?

3. Have you ever served somewhere and really felt moved by what God accomplished? Could God be inviting you to join Him in the work He is doing there?

4. In his book, <u>Experiencing God</u>, Henry Blackaby said, "God is always at work. Look around you and see what God is doing. [14] Then feel free to join in." What work do you see God engaged in around you, at your church, in your community?

5. Are there any specific ministries for which God has gifted you? What are you passionate about? What turns you on?

6. Will you determine in your heart that you will seek the next step in God's will for your life and be open to His every leading? It means you will have to surrender your time and be ready to engage.

Memory Verse:

Matthew 7:21 *"Not everyone who says to me, 'Lord, Lord,' will enter the kingdom of heaven, but only he who does the will of my Father who is in heaven."*

How to Pray

Jesus' disciples asked Jesus how to pray and He gave them, by way of example, the Lord's Prayer. **Read Matthew 6:9-13.**

The Lord's Prayer was meant to be an example of how to pray, not a prayer that should be repeated over and over and over without thinking about what it means. Prayer is conversation with God. You should spend time listening, as well as talking. An easy way to pray is to follow the P.R.A.Y. acronym.

P stands for "praise." You should start your prayer with praise to God, acknowledging His greatness and overflowing with gratitude. Psalm 100:4 says, *"Enter his gates with thanksgiving and his courts with praise."*

R stands for "requests." Only after you have your mind focused on Him, rather than yourself, and have thanked God for His beautiful creation, His blessings in your life, and for even caring about your small concerns, then it is OK to ask Him to take care of what is troubling you.

A stands for "agree with God." While you're in conversation with God, He may lay on your heart an area of your life He wants you to change or a sin you need to confess. Right away you may focus on someone else you think God must be talking about. No, God is talking to you. He is not a gossip. Rather than make excuses, agree with God and think about how you can make those changes in your life.

Y stands for "say Yes." If God asks you to do something, do not make excuses. Do not say, "I won't," or "I can't." Simply say "Yes" to what He is asking you to do, and then do it as soon as possible.

Some Prayer Principles

God wants you to place your burdens upon Him. Don't think you're bothering God with your petty problems. He actually delights in taking the burden off of you and placing it upon Himself (Matthew 11:28-30).

First humble yourself before God. God wants you to come before Him realizing you are unworthy and having a broken heart over your sin (Psalm 51:17).

Pray bold prayers. The God who created the universe is able to handle anything you can throw at Him. Do not put Him in a box by constraining what He can do.

Pray persistently (Luke 18:7-8). If your prayer is not answered immediately, God wants you to be persistent in coming back to Him with your request until it is answered or you receive a clear "No."

Pray specific prayers. You won't really know how wonderfully God answered your prayer unless you pray for specific things.

Pray scripture. God cannot lie and His word stands forever. Psalm 119:89 says, *"Your word, O Lord, is eternal; it stands firm in the heavens."* When you pray scripture, you are saying to God that you have faith in His word, that you believe God's word is true, and that you trust Him to be faithful to His word. The enemy knows the power of the word is stronger than he.

Pray expectant prayers. When you ask God for something, you have to have faith that He is going to answer your request. If you do not really think He will grant it, He will not, because He requires that you have faith (James 1:6).

Let go of unforgiveness. Jesus said if you are praying to God and then you remember that you have a strained relationship with someone, go and resolve the issue, then come back to prayer (Matthew 5:23).

Pray "in the name of Jesus." Jesus said in John 14:13, *"I will do whatever you ask in my name, so that the Son may bring glory to the Father."* By praying "in Jesus' name" we bring glory to the Father, and we call on the mighty power of Jesus' name. Jesus is your power of attorney. When we pray in the name of Jesus, we are stating that we are under the authority of Jesus. The mention of His name makes the enemy cringe.

When presenting your requests, pray with someone else. In Matthew 18:19, Jesus said, *"If two of you on earth agree about anything you ask for, it will be done for you by my Father in heaven."*

When seeking God's presence, go into a quiet place and get alone with God (Matthew 6:6). Just have a conversation with God.

APPLICATION:

1. Based on the following verses, what should your response be when God answers prayer? Psalm 28:6-7 says, *"Praise be to the Lord, for he has heard my cry for mercy. The Lord is my strength and my shield; my heart trusts in him, and I am helped. My heart leaps for joy and I will give thanks to him in song."*

2. God hears all our prayers. Sometimes He doesn't answer them the way we want them to be answered because He knows what is best for us. Sometimes He just tells us no, perhaps because our request is a selfish one. Sometimes God takes awhile to answer our prayers; perhaps He wants us to develop faith and learn to be persistent in coming to Him. Sometimes our prayers are hindered because our behavior is less than Christ-like. However, often our prayers will be answered immediately and in ways we did not expect. But know that God hears all our prayers and has our best interests at heart. Never stop believing for a miracle.

3. Do you want answered prayer? Check out these verses in Psalm 58:6-9. *"Is not this the kind of fasting I have chosen: to loose the chains of injustice and untie the cords of the yoke, to*

set the oppressed free and break every yoke? Is it not to share your food with the hungry and to provide the poor wanderer with shelter—when you see the naked, to clothe him, and not to turn away from your own flesh and blood? Then your light will break forth like the dawn, and your healing will quickly appear; then your righteousness will go before you, and the glory of the Lord will be your rear guard. Then you will call, <u>and the Lord will answer</u>; you will cry for help, and he will say: Here am I."

Memory Verse:

Philippians 4:6-7 *"Do not be anxious about anything, but in everything, by prayer and petition, with thanksgiving, present your requests to God. And the peace of God, which transcends all understanding, will guard your hearts and your minds in Christ Jesus."*

God's Judgment

2 Corinthians 5:10 says, *"For we must all appear before the judg-ment seat of Christ, that each one may receive what is due him for the things done while in the body, whether good or bad."* That's right. When you die, you will stand before God and account for how you lived your life on earth. The Bible says there will be separate judg-ments for nonbelievers and believers. The nonbelievers will be asked what they did about Jesus, and how they lived their lives, whether for themselves or for others. The believers will be accountable for how well they fulfilled God's will for their lives, with the answer deter-mining what kind of reward they receive. Revelation 20:11-12 talks about two sets of books being opened: the Book of Life and the Book of Deeds. Your name is entered in the Book of Life when you take that all-important first step of inviting Jesus into your life to be the leader of your life. Revelation 20:15 tells us, *"If anyone's name was not found written in the book of life, he was thrown into the lake of fire."*

The second book to be opened is the Book of Deeds. If you truly love Jesus, your life will be full of expressions of your love for Him, where you readily volunteered your time, talents, and treasure to advance God's kingdom on earth. Just as you cannot enter Heaven without your name being in the Book of Life, likewise you would ex-pect that there would be some evidence of having produced fruit for God, recorded in the Book of Deeds.

Read 1 Corinthians 3:11-15 on evaluating our good deeds.

This passage explains how a believer's deeds will be evaluated. Only the right kind of work will be rewarded. First, our good deeds have to be built upon the foundation of Jesus Christ. His death on the cross and His resurrection from the grave are the cornerstone on which His church is to be built. Any works built upon any other premise, or for anyone else's glory, will not count. The passage goes on to explain that the quality of our good deeds will be evaluated. Those of high quality (represented by gold, silver, and costly stones) are rewarded, while those of low quality (represented by wood, hay, or straw) are destroyed. High quality deeds include telling others about Jesus, building up believers, teaching the word of God with accurate doctrine, ministering to the needy, completing the work He gave us to do, and living a Christian life that models the life of Christ. Our deeds will be tested through the fire of God's justice. If they survive the test, we will receive our just reward. If our deeds are partially burned, we will suffer loss of rewards, but still be permitted into heaven.

Part of God's evaluation of our good deeds will be to examine our motives. In 1 Corinthians 4:5, the Bible says, *"He will bring to light what is hidden in darkness and will expose the motives of men's hearts."* So for example, if you served as a carpenter building homes for Habitat for Humanity because it looked good on your resume and helped you to get elected as the town mayor, then that was service for you, and not for God. Galatians 1:10 asks, *"Am I now trying to win the approval of men, or of God? Or am I trying to please men? If I were still trying to please men, I would not be a servant of Christ."*

The bottom line is this: When we truly grasp how much God did for us when He sent His son to die on the cross for us, when we realize how much He loves us, then our lives will overflow with good works. If you do not feel that way, try spending more time developing your relationship with the creator and getting to know Him better.

APPLICATION:

1. **Read Luke 7:36-47 the story of the woman who was forgiven much.**

   Ephesians 2:10 says, *"For we are God's workmanship, created in Christ Jesus to do good works, which God prepared in advance for us to do."* We were created by God to do good works. As the architect of His creation, God decided that He would work through people to administer His love to His creation. What an incredible privilege, responsibility, and opportunity to be given that kind of worth by our creator! Also, as part of His design, He gave us free will to either embrace or reject that privilege. Since God loves to give gifts to His children, He told us ahead of time that rewards would be available for all those who embrace His concept of serving others. We should not be motivated to serve others purely for our selfish reward; but we should be motivated to serve out of love for what God did to redeem us from sin. Jesus touched on this principle in Luke 7:36-47. The woman who had been forgiven much expressed that forgiveness in a very demonstrative show of love to her Master. Someone who has been forgiven much will love much, and someone who has been forgiven little may love little. So will you take the time to focus on just how much Jesus did for you on the cross, so you can love much?

2. If God lays out a plan for our lives while we are still in the womb (Psalm 139:16), then He will also lay out a reward for having completed that plan. If we fail to complete all or part of His plan for our life, then we will lose all or part of our reward. 2 John 8 says, *"Watch out that you do not lose what you have worked for, but that you may be rewarded fully."* Is there any part of God's plan for your life that you are knowingly neglecting?

3. What will we do with these rewards anyway? Obviously we do not wear them around heaven saying to everyone, "Look at me. See how good I was!" Revelation 4:10 gives the answer.

There will be times where we worship Jesus in heaven and we will lay our crowns at His feet, symbolic of our earthly service having been all for Him. Will you have something to offer to your king?

4. Joshua, a courageous man of God, embraced serving God when he spoke before his people. In Joshua 24:15, he said, *"But if serving the Lord seems undesirable to you, then choose for yourselves this day whom you will serve, whether the gods your forefathers served beyond the River, or the gods of the Amorites, in whose land you are living. But as for me and my household, we will serve the Lord."* Whom will you serve?

5. If God is speaking anything to you through this lesson, record it in the appendix.

Memory Verse:

Ephesians 2:10 *"For we are God's workmanship, created in Christ Jesus to do good works, which God prepared in advance for us to do."*

God's Reward

The apostle Paul referred to the rewards we will receive as crowns. He depicted them as a victor's wreath, given to athletes who won the Olympic events that were contested in his day. The disciple John also spoke of crowns as being the reward given to us by God. In the previous lesson we learned that these crowns will be laid at the feet of Jesus to honor Him for His sacrifice on the cross. Both Paul and John visited heaven (see 2 Corinthians 12:1-6 and Revelation 1:2) and both mentioned physical crowns as rewards given by God.

Five crowns are mentioned in the bible. They are as follows:

1. **The Crown of Glory**, given to those who were shepherds of God's church, whether elders, or deacons, or small group shepherds.

    1 Peter 5:1-4 says, *"To the elders among you . . . be shepherds of God's flock that is under your care, serving as overseers—not because you must, but because you are willing, as God wants you to be; not greedy for money but eager to serve; not lording it over those entrusted to you, but being examples to the flock. And when the Chief Shepherd appears, you will receive the crown of glory that will never fade away."*

2. **The Crown of Life**, given to those who endure difficult trials or persecution without turning their back on God.

James 1:12 says, *"Blessed is the man who perseveres under trial, because when he has stood the test, he will receive the crown of life that God has promised to those who love him."*

Revelation 2:10 says, *"Do not be afraid of what you are about to suffer. I tell you, the devil will put some of you in prison to test you, and you will suffer persecution for ten days. Be faithful, even to the point of death, and I will give you the crown of life."*

3. **The Everlasting Crown**, given to those who through strict discipline and training strive for excellence and faithfulness in their spiritual walk.

1 Corinthians 9:25 says, *"Everyone who competes in the games goes into strict training. They do it to get a crown that will not last; but we do it to get a crown that will last forever."*

4. **The Crown of Righteousness**, given to those who complete the work that God has prepared for them to do, and serve Him all their days.

2 Timothy 4:7-8 says, *"I have fought the good fight, I have finished the race, I have kept the faith. Now there is in store for me the crown of righteousness, which the Lord, the righteous Judge, will award to me on that day—and not only to me, but also to all who have longed for his appearing."*

It is important to note that the concept of retiring at age 65 to live on a golf course and never work again is not found in the Bible. Paul wrote, "I have finished the race," when he knew his death was near.

5. **The Crown of Rejoicing** with the Saved, given to those who lead someone to Christ, or disciple someone to lead them to maturity in their faith.

1 Thessalonians 2:19-20 says, *"For what is our hope, our joy, or the crown in which we will glory in the presence of our Lord Jesus when he comes? Is it not you? Indeed, you are our glory and joy."*

Other ways to be rewarded that are mentioned in the Bible are as follows:

1. for sacrificing time with family in order to serve God.

    Matthew 19:29 says, *"And everyone who has left houses or brothers or sisters or father or mother or children or fields for my sake will receive a hundred times as much and will inherit eternal life."*

2. for treating your enemies with kindness.

    Luke 6:35 says, *"But love your enemies, do good to them, and lend to them without expecting to get anything back. Then your reward will be great, and you will be sons of the Most High."*

3. for being generous for Christ.

    1 Timothy 6:17-19 says, *"Command those who are rich in this present world not to be arrogant nor to put their hope in wealth, which is so uncertain, but to put their hope in God, who richly provides us with everything for our enjoyment. Command them to do good, to be rich in good deeds, and to be generous and willing to share. In this way they will lay up treasure for themselves as a firm foundation for the coming age, so that they may take hold of the life that is truly life."*

4. for showing hospitality or aid to other believers.

    Mark 9:41 says, *"I tell you the truth, anyone who gives you a cup of water in my name because you belong to Christ will certainly not lose his reward."*

5. for caring for the poor.

Luke 14:13-14 says, *"But when you give a banquet, invite the poor, the crippled, the lame, the blind, and you will be blessed. Although they cannot repay you, you will be repaid at the resurrection of the righteous."*

You can tell from reading about these rewards that Jesus' heart was for people. Yes, you can serve God by taking care of the church grounds and building, or taking up the offering during church, but the rewards mentioned here are for the difficult task of getting involved in peoples' lives and making a difference.

What is our biggest obstacle to attaining rewards? Of course, it is time. We are selfish with our time and want to do what we want to do. Satan will work to fill our lives with busyness so we don't have time to serve God. If we look at a budget of our time, we will find many wasted hours each day that could have been put to better use. Ephesians 5:15-16 says, *"Be very careful, then, how you live—not as unwise but as wise, making the most of every opportunity, because the days are evil."*

APPLICATION:

1. The apostle Paul, in Philippians 3:14, said his goal was to *"win the prize for which God has called me heavenward in Christ Jesus."* I challenge you to consider what God has called you to do and pray about how you can complete that calling with excellence, so that God has in store for you a crown. Maybe it's the Everlasting Crown. Discipline yourself to spend time in the word each morning and meditate on what you read. Set aside part of that time to talk to God. Spend time studying your bible, and this book, in the evening. Maybe it's the Crown of Rejoicing with the Saved. Go through this book with other believers to disciple them and tell them about Christ.

2. Will you ask God to give you a passion for serving the poor, the downtrodden, the hopeless, the forgotten, or the lost? Why not set aside a few hours each week to serve Him by serving them?

3. In 1 Corinthians 9:24, Paul said, *"Do you not know that in a race all the runners run, but only one gets the prize? Run in such a way as to get the prize."* Paul was cautioning us not to take our service to God lightly, as something we do only when we feel like it or have nothing else better to do. On the other hand, it is not something we should do in our own strength. We should be motivated to do an excellent job; it is the Lord we are serving. We should be motivated that God receive the glory, not us. And we should be cooperating with the Holy Spirit, following that still small voice, to ensure that we complete God's will and not our will. Then your service will be totally pleasing to God and result in a crown given to you when you stand before Him.

Memory Verse:

1 Corinthians 9:25 *"Everyone who competes in the games goes into strict training. They do it to get a crown that will not last; but we do it to get a crown that will last forever."*

Giving

Key Principle: God wants you to honor Him with your money and not worship it.

The Bible says in Luke 12:34, *"Where your treasure is, there your heart will be also."* Our attitude toward giving is a reflection of our hearts. If our hearts are full of desire for earthly treasure, we most likely will not be giving generously to God. If our hearts are full of love for God and a desire to advance His kingdom on earth, our money will flow freely to God.

In Matthew 6:24b, Jesus said, *"You cannot serve both God and Money."* There are many things in the world to compete for your money: homes, cars, education, clothes, jewelry, travel. Don't be divided in your mind about your giving to God. He should have first place in your heart.

How to Give

When it comes to giving, <u>how</u> we give is more important than <u>how much</u> we give.

2 Corinthians 9:7 says, *"Each man should give what he has decided in his heart to give, not reluctantly or under compulsion, for God loves a cheerful giver."* When someone tells you how much you should give, you may start to feel obligated and ask yourself, "How much do I owe?" This attitude will quickly take the joy out of giving.

Besides giving cheerfully, God wants us to give to Him first. Proverbs 3:9 says, *"Honor the Lord with your wealth, with the first fruits of all your crops."* God doesn't want the leftovers, what's left in your wallet at the end of the week after you've enjoyed spending your money on yourself. So you should decide how much you want to give out of each paycheck, and then give that amount to God when you are paid.

Besides giving to God first, He wants us to give sacrificially. For that reason, the Old Testament guideline was a hefty ten percent. Based on what you make and what your expenses are for basic necessities, just giving five percent may be a hardship and a sacrifice. When you are older and earning good money, you may be able to give ten percent with no problem. In that case, you should give more than ten percent.

Key Principle: We are to be good and faithful stewards of all that God has given us.

A steward is someone who takes care of another person's property. As stewards of God's property (the money, property, and talent He has given to us) we are required to be faithful in our giving back to God and to invest wisely in the work of His kingdom.

1 Corinthians 4:2 says, *"Now it is required that those who have been given a trust must prove faithful."*

Read Matthew 25:14-30, the parable of the talents.

In Matthew 25, Jesus discusses two parables. Both are about Heaven, as He mentions in chapter 25 verse 1. The second parable, which is discussed in verses 14-30, is about being a good steward of what God has entrusted to you. The first man was given five talents and put his money to work and earned five more. The second man was given two talents and earned two more. Both received the same reward: they heard "Well done" from the Father, were given some responsibility for their faithfulness, and shared in their Master's happiness. But the third man had nothing to show for the money that was entrusted to him. He met the Master's wrath and was thrown out of the kingdom into darkness, where he experienced weeping and gnashing of teeth.

What is the meaning of this parable? Whether you earn $2,000. or $2,000,000., you are rewarded in Heaven based on the degree of your generosity. But if you have <u>nothing</u> to show for your stewardship of the money God has given you on earth, you will be punished. Since our attitude about giving is a reflection of our hearts, obviously the third man had no love for God in his heart, and was not permitted into God's kingdom.

Don't Spend Beyond Your Means

1 Corinthians 7:23 says, *"You were bought at a price; do not become slaves of men."* When we are in debt, we are slaves to our creditors. God wants us to be indebted only to Him. [15] Running up a large credit card debt, because we cannot afford what we desire, indicates a lack of contentment, impatience with what we perceive as God's lack of provision for us, and the sin of covetousness in our lives. God will provide for your needs in His timing.

APPLICATION:

1. What is the hardest part to come to terms with about giving your money away?

2. God requires us to be faithful stewards. If you are working, start giving. If you are not making any money, start working, as Ephesians 4:28 says, so *"that he may have something to share with those in need."* If God has blessed you financially, He expects you to be blessing others. If He has richly blessed you, He expects you to be giving back even more. God wants you to honor Him in the way you give and how much you give. Are you being faithful with what God has given to you?

3. In order to give, a family has to live on less that what they are bringing in each month. A budget will help get your family expenses under control so that you can "afford" to give. If

you desire to give but feel like you have little to offer God, that's even better. You will get to see God at work performing miracles in your finances, and praises to God will flow forth from your lips.

4. Debt can be a sickness, and credit cards make it easy to get sick. If you have an outstanding balance on your credit cards, you are paying a hefty surcharge on the items that you purchased. Will you consider paying off your credit card debt as soon as possible?

5. If you have resolved to make any changes to your finances, record them in the appendix.

Memory Verse:

1 Corinthians 4:2 *"Now it is required that those who have been given a trust must prove faithful."*

Stewardship

Key Principle: God tests our stewardship of our money. If we pass the test, he entrusts us with more.

Luke 16:10 says, *"Whoever can be trusted with very little can also be trusted with much, and whoever is dishonest with very little will also be dishonest with much."* God will test you, starting when you are just earning a small amount of money. It's hard to give to God when you can barely make ends meet. But if you realize God is testing your faithfulness to give back to Him, you will give sacrificially. God will notice that you have been faithful (or dishonest) with little, and reward you (or not) by entrusting more to you. Matthew 25:15 reminds us that each of the three men in the parable of the talents was initially granted money, "each according to his ability." Ability to do what? The ability to be faithful stewards with their money. Spoken another way, when you have proven yourself faithful to give back to God, He is even more generous right back at you. Luke 6:38 says, *"Give, and it will be given to you. A good measure, pressed down, shaken together and running over, will be poured into your lap. For with the measure you use, it will be measured to you."*

If God richly blesses the faithful giver, why aren't we all enjoying His bountiful blessings? Because we have not taken the first step to trust that what He promises will be true <u>for me</u>. If you trust His promises, you will be generous even when you can't see how you are going to pay your bills. But you have to take the first step and act in trust.

Wealth

Is being wealthy an evil thing? Deuteronomy 8:18 says, *"But remember the Lord your God, for it is he who gives you the ability to produce wealth, and so confirms his covenant, which he swore to your forefathers."* Many of the great men of the Old Testament—Abraham, Isaac, Jacob, Joseph, David, Solomon, and Job were all wealthy. God swore to abundantly bless our obedience to Him, in Deuteronomy 28. If you have wealth, enjoy it, and be thankful to God.

But wealth can wind up being a snare for many believers when they stop using it to further God's kingdom on earth and start hoarding it. James 5:1 tells us if you hoard your money you should *"weep and wail because of the misery that is coming upon you."*

What if I am not hoarding my money, I am just spending it all on myself? The following parable addresses that.

Read Luke 12:16-21, the parable of the greedy rich man.

In this parable, a farmer was so blessed that he kept building bigger barns to store his grain. Then, after he had accumulated more than he would ever need, he decided to reward himself and take it easy. Then God suddenly took his life. "What's wrong with that?" you ask, "That is every man's dream." The problem is found in verse 21. <u>The man stored up things for himself without being rich toward God.</u> Listen, the day will never come when you stand before God and lament, "I should have kept more for myself." Instead you'll be saying, "If only I had done more for God." Jesus gave the warning at the start of this parable, in Luke 12:15. *"Watch out! Be on your guard against all kinds of greed; a man's life does not consist in the abundance of his possessions."*

Key Principle: You reap what you sow.

Not only will God reward our faithfulness in giving by giving back to us, but when we are very generous in our giving, that invokes God's generosity back at us.

2 Corinthians 9:6 says, *"Whoever sows generously will also reap generously."* And God's generosity far exceeds our definition of generosity. Additionally, 2 Corinthians 9:8 says, *"God is able to make all grace abound to you, so that in all things, at all times, having all that you need, you will abound in every good work."* This verse says that not only will we be supplied with all we need, but we will have extra income to give to every cause God places on our heart. So we really have no excuse for not being generous.

APPLICATION:

1. You should not give in order to receive. You should give to be obedient to God and to honor Him. However, if you have doubts about God's faithfulness to honor you back, the Bible says you can test God on this principle. In Malachi 3:10 God speaks through the prophet Malachi and challenges His people to pay their full tithe, ten percent of their income. *"Bring the whole tithe into the storehouse, that there may be food in my house. Test me in this,"* says the Lord Almighty, *"and see if I will not throw open the floodgates of heaven and pour out so much blessing that you will not have room enough for it."*

2. I challenge you to be praying about how much God wants you to give. If you are giving one percent of your income now, you might gradually step it up each year until you are giving more and more. You might pray a prayer like this: God, I don't know how I can increase my giving but I do know I want You to be glorified greatly through me. I want to have a role in your kingdom's work on earth. I want to be the hands and feet of Christ. So please help me to manage my money faithfully. Help me to be satisfied with what You have given me. Take away my desire to catch up to my neighbors. Keep me out of debt, keep me honest in all my financial transactions, and bless me financially so that I can be a blessing to

others. Acting in faith, I am increasing my giving by this small percentage to show that I trust that you will make it happen. Keep me faithful in my giving. I want my financial gift to be honoring to you. In Jesus' name. Amen.

3. Will you vow to live within your means, that is, on less than you make? Give to God first, set aside some for savings, and live on the rest. As you get promotions, pay increases, or year-end bonuses, do not quickly expand your lifestyle to absorb your increase. First increase the amount you are giving to God until you are tithing, then increase your savings, and then finally spend money on yourself.

4. Keep you eye on the goal. God will reward a lifetime of giving to Him. If He is delighted by how you honor Him financially, He will give back to you generously in His timing and you will not lack for anything. Matthew 6:33 says, *"But seek first his kingdom and his righteousness, and all these things will be given to you as well."*

5. Remember, when God abundantly blesses you, He wants to do even greater works through you, to enlarge your harvest. 2 Corinthians 9:10 says, *"Now he who supplies seed to the sower and bread for food will also supply and increase your store of seed and will enlarge the harvest of your righteousness."*

Memory Verse:

Matthew 6:33 *"But seek first his kingdom and his righteousness, and all these things will be given to you as well."*

Week 5

The Holy Spirit

After Jesus' resurrection, and before He was taken up to Heaven, He told His disciples to wait for the promised Holy Spirit (Acts 1:4). A number of weeks later, when thousands of people from across the Mediterranean world were in Jerusalem for the celebration of Pentecost, the Holy Spirit showed up. Acts 2 describes it like the sound of a violent wind. Flames of fire appeared on the heads of all the disciples and they began preaching to the crowd. Each person heard the message in his own language. They were amazed and perplexed, not sure how they could be hearing Galileans speaking in foreign tongues. On that day, 3000 people decided to follow Jesus. Peter healed a crippled man, and other miracles began to happen. The word of Jesus' resurrection from the dead spread like wildfire, even though there was no television, radio, newspaper, or internet. Eventually, the entire Mediterranean world heard about Jesus in that first century after His death.

The Holy Spirit is the third person of the Godhead, the three-in-one God, which consists of God the Father, God the Son and God the Holy Spirit. The Holy Spirit is not an "it," but a person. Jesus referred to Him as "He" (John 16:13). When we first invite Jesus into our hearts, the Holy Spirit takes up residence in our bodies. 1 Corinthians 6:19-20 says, *"Do you not know that your body is a temple of the Holy Spirit, who is in you, whom you have received from God? You are not your own; you were bought at a price. Therefore honor God with your body."*

Some roles of the Holy Spirit are the following:

1. He helps us to understand the truth of the scriptures. He is our teacher who reveals the word of God to our hearts. John 16:13 says, *"But when he, the Spirit of truth, comes, he will guide you into all truth. He will not speak on his own; he will speak only what he hears, and he will tell you what is yet to come."* When we dive into the word, we need to ask the Holy Spirit for help in understanding it.

2. He helps us to communicate with God in prayer. Romans 8:26 says, *"We do not know what we ought to pray for, but the Spirit himself intercedes for us with groans that words cannot express."* Ask the Spirit to join you in prayer.

3. The Holy Spirit convicts the <u>saved</u> of their sin in order to bring them back into a right relationship with God. Ezekiel 36:27 says, *"And I will put my Spirit in you and move you to follow my decrees and be careful to keep my laws."* When the Holy Spirit convicts us of sin, we should confess our sin, repent (change), and if we have offended someone, make restitution.

4. He convicts the <u>unsaved</u> of their sin in order to help draw them to Christ. John 16:8 says, *"When he comes, he will convict the world of guilt in regard to sin and righteousness and judgment."*

5. The Holy Spirit does the work to bring an unsaved person into a saving relationship with Jesus Christ. John 3: 5-6 says, *"I tell you the truth, no one can enter the kingdom of God unless he is born of water and the Spirit. Flesh gives birth to flesh, but the Spirit gives birth to spirit."* 1 Corinthians 12:3 says, *"No one can say 'Jesus is Lord' except by the Holy Spirit."*

6. He gives us power to speak to others about Jesus. Acts 1:8 says, *"But you will receive power when the Holy Spirit comes upon you; and you will be my witnesses in Jerusalem, and in all Judea and Samaria, and to the ends of the earth."* We can see in items 4-6 that the Spirit is at work to bring the lost to Jesus. Now it is our role to join in and share our testimony, share the gospel, and lead them in a prayer to receive Jesus as their Lord and Savior.

7. He searches the thoughts of God the Father to reveal His plan for our lives. 1 Corinthians 2:10b-11 says, *"The Spirit searches all things, even the deep things of God. For who among men knows the thoughts of a man except the man's spirit within him? In the same way no one knows the thoughts of God except the Spirit of God."* When the Holy Spirit asks us to take some small step toward serving God, we need to say yes and then join in with what God is doing.

8. The Holy Spirit constantly praises Jesus. During Jesus' ride into Jerusalem on Palm Sunday, the Pharisees told Jesus to rebuke His followers for praising Him. They argued that such praise could only be given to God. In Luke 19:40, Jesus responded, *"'I tell you,' he replied, 'if they keep quiet, the stones will cry out.'"* Jesus meant that the Holy Spirit was at work and would not be silenced.

9. The Holy Spirit gives spiritual gifts to all believers. 1 Corinthians 12:7-11 says, *"Now to each one the manifestation of the Spirit is given for the common good. To one there is given through the Spirit the message of wisdom, to another the message of knowledge by means of the same Spirit, to another faith by the same Spirit, to another gifts of healing by that one Spirit, to another miraculous powers, to another prophecy, to another distinguishing between spirits, to another speaking in*

different kinds of tongues, and to still another the interpreta-tion of tongues. All these are the work of one and the same Spirit, and he gives them to each one, just as he determines."

Do You Feel His Presence?

Sometimes you may strongly feel the Holy Spirit's presence in your life, and at other times you may wonder where He went. We can diminish the Holy Spirit's presence several ways.

First, the Bible says in 1 Thessalonians 5:19, *"Do not <u>put out</u> the Spirit's fire."* We do that when we ignore the promptings of the Holy Spirit. If the Holy Spirit prompts us to pray for someone, invite someone to church, or tell someone about Jesus, for example, and we ignore Him, we are putting out the Spirit's fire and extinguishing His power in our lives. We need to give Him complete control in our lives.

Secondly, Ephesians 4:30 tells us not to <u>grieve</u> the Holy Spirit. We can grieve the Holy Spirit through any sinful action that goes against the new nature that is within us. By harboring unforgiveness toward someone, slandering someone, being rebellious, or just holding on to our favorite sin, we cause the Holy Spirit to feel deep sadness or distress which silences Him in our beings.

Thirdly, in Acts 7:31, Stephen spoke to the crowd and called them stubborn people for <u>resisting</u> the Holy Spirit. Some people may know that the Holy Spirit is trying to bring them to Christ, but their pride will keep them from accepting Him as Lord and Savior. This constant stubbornness makes it that much harder to later come to Christ.

Finally, Matthew 12:31-32 tells us not to <u>blaspheme</u> the Holy Spirit, and that blasphemy against the Holy Spirit will not be forgiven. Since it is the Holy Spirit's role to lead us to Christ by convicting us of our sin, to reject that conviction of sin (and ultimately reject Jesus) is to blaspheme the Holy Spirit.

Being Filled with the Holy Spirit

We already discussed that when you ask Jesus to be the Lord of your life, the Holy Spirit takes up residence in you. But beyond just residing in you, Paul commanded believers to *"Be filled with the Spirit"* (Ephesians 5:18). The Holy Spirit fills you up when you cooperate with Him in all His roles mentioned above. He exists to help us have fellowship with God, so we should be spending daily time in the word and in prayer. He exists to guide us and let us know when we have sinned, so we should have a repentant heart and desire to follow Him first, rather than following the world. He exists to draw the lost to Christ, so we should join in partnership with Him to tell others about Jesus. He exists to reveal God's plan for our lives, so we should be obedient to follow His leading. He exists to magnify the name of Jesus, so we should be filled with praise for Jesus every day of our lives. And He exists to give us spiritual gifts, so we should be exercising those gifts. When you are doing these things, the Holy Spirit will be vibrant within you.

The Holy Spirit will entrust you with little things to determine your faithfulness, how you will obey. [16] If you give up doing what you want to do, and instead do what He wants you to do, He will know you can be entrusted with more: more empowering, more revealing of His word, more revealing of His will for you, more fellowship with Him, more correction, more guidance, and more filling of your heart. His anointing will then be upon you to help you fulfill the calling He has placed upon you.

APPLICATION:

1. Be careful that you do not treat irreverently the power of the Holy Spirit. Hebrews 10:29 says, *"How much more severely do you think a man deserves to be punished who has trampled the Son of God under foot, who has treated as an unholy thing the blood of the covenant that sanctified him, and who has <u>insulted the Spirit</u> of grace?"*

2. Isaiah 30:21 says, *"Whether you turn to the right or to the left, your ears will hear a voice behind you saying, 'This is the way; walk in it.'"* What do you do when you hear that voice? Do you disregard it and do what you want to do, or do you say,

"Yes" to God? The more you obey the Spirit, the greater is His presence and power in your life. If you say no to the Spirit, you will quench His fire, and then you will cease to hear His voice.

3. Do you feel the Holy Spirit is vibrant in your life today? If not, what might you be doing to silence Him?

Memory Verse:

1 Thessalonians 5:19 *"Do not put out the Spirit's fire."*

The Power of the Holy Spirit

Key Principle: God delegates power, through the Holy Spirit, in those who believe and invoke the name of Jesus.

In Ephesians 1:19, Paul prays that our hearts may be opened in order to know of *"his incomparably great power for us who believe."*

This power is available to those who have the Holy Spirit living in them and have faith that His word is true. Mark 16: 17-18 says, *"And these signs will accompany <u>those who believe</u>: <u>In my name</u> they will drive out demons; they will speak in new tongues; . . . they will place their hands on sick people, and they will get well."* This amazing ability is available to those who believe and who call on the name of Jesus, and will be increasingly evident when the Holy Spirit is poured out in the end times. Joel 2:28 says, *" . . . I will pour out my Spirit on all people. Your sons and daughters will prophesy, your old men will dream dreams, your young men will see visions."* You may think, "This is not the kind of power I'm seeking. I want to have the power to change someone's life for the better. I want people to see Jesus in me and desire to know Him for themselves. I want the power to clearly communicate the gospel so I can lead others to Christ." Jesus said in John 14:12, *"I tell you the truth, anyone who <u>has faith in me</u> will do what I have been doing. He will do even greater things than these."* This ability is available to those who have great faith. This ability comes through the Holy Spirit and Luke 11:13 teaches that the

Holy Spirit is given to those who ask the Father. *"If you then, though you are evil, know how to give good gifts to your children, how much more will your Father in heaven give the Holy Spirit to those who ask him!"* We already talked about how we can grieve the Holy Spirit or put out the Spirit's fire. This ability is only available in those who have a vibrant Spirit within them, who are cooperating with the Holy Spirit.

Of course, I need to mention that spiritual gifts are distributed to all believers in accordance with God's will. 1 Corinthians 12:28 says, *"And in the church God has appointed first of all apostles, second prophets, third teachers, then workers of miracles, also those having gifts of healing, those able to help others, those with gifts of administration, and those speaking in different kinds of tongues."* The apostle Paul, in 1 Corinthians 12:12-31, likens the church to a human body. Just as the body is composed of many organs working in unison, the church is composed of people with different spiritual gifts acting together as one body. If you do not belong to a church, one that God has led you to join, then some church is trying to operate without all of its parts present.

Key Principle: Because we are under Jesus' authority, we can exercise that authority.
Read Luke 7: 1-10, the story of the centurion with the sick servant.

A centurion whose servant was dying sent word to some of the elders of the Jews, asking if they would send Jesus to come heal his servant. So Jesus started out toward the centurion's house. When he was not far off, the centurion said, "Lord, don't trouble yourself, for I do not deserve to have you come under my roof. That is why I did not even consider myself worthy to come to you. But say the word, and my servant will be healed. For I myself am a man under authority, with soldiers under me. I tell this one, 'Go,' and he goes; and that one 'Come,' and he comes." Jesus heard this and was amazed. This man understands authority. Because he is under Caesar's authority, he acts with Caesar's authority and can exercise that authority. The principle is this: because we are under the authority of Jesus, we can act with Jesus' authority and can exercise that authority. So exercise it! *"For the kingdom of God is not a matter of talk but of power"* (1 Corinthians 4:20). In Luke 10:19, Jesus said, *"I have given you authority to trample on snakes and scorpions* (these were demonic symbols) *and to overcome all the power of the enemy; nothing will harm you."* Use it.

In Matthew 28:18, Jesus said, *"All authority in heaven and on earth has been given to me. Therefore go . . ."* Jesus delegated His authority to us in order to fill us with the supernatural power of the Holy Spirit, that we might fill the earth with His glory.

Key Principle: Jesus wants followers who are passionate for Him and will follow Him without any reservations.
Read Luke 14:28-33.

A man does not take on a project to build a tower without first considering the cost. He must also plan for contingencies in case something goes wrong. Jesus is saying, in the two examples in the above passage, that He wants us to carefully consider the cost of full commitment to Him in a lifetime of service. Pursuing a life of service to Jesus may cost you in terms of a lower salary than some other occupation might bring you. It may cost you in leisure time with your family. It may cost you in friends, influence, lifestyle, and even cause immense sacrifice. When you encounter setbacks, if you are not fully committed, you may throw in the towel altogether. But if you have considered the cost, you will be able to stay committed and see God's calling through to completion.

The cost for having a vibrant, intimate relationship with the Most High God is to deny yourself daily (Luke 9:23). In John 10:27, Jesus said, *"My sheep listen to my voice; I know them, and they follow me."* If you know Him, you should hear His voice and be fully obedient to drop what you are doing to follow His call.

In Luke 9:57-62, Jesus rebuffed several would-be followers who came to Him with some reservations. He did not want followers who would refrain from giving their all because of concerns about comfort, about settling their father's estate, or about their family. He doesn't want us to follow Him while having any reservations. What will my family and friends say about me? What if God calls me to some place I don't want to go? What if I am not up to the task? What will this do to my career? God wants us to be "all in." He does not want us looking over our shoulder and wondering what might have been. He does not want us turning back at the first sign of trouble. He does not want us holding anything back. He does not want us to give in when we are persecuted. In short, He wants us to be fully prepared to give up everything to follow Him.

APPLICATION:

1. If you believe what Jesus said about believers having great power, you will start praying boldly for people to be healed from sickness, for Satan to be gone, for demonic chains to be broken, for deliverance to be granted, for relationships to be healed. The first recorded prayer of the early church called on God for healing. In Acts 4:30, Peter and John called on God to, "Stretch out your hand to heal and perform miraculous signs and wonders through the name of your holy servant Jesus." "I do not know if I can do that," you may be thinking. "What if I lay hands on someone and pray for healing in the name of Jesus and nothing happens?" Do not be discouraged if you don't see immediate results. The power of the Holy Spirit is still at work through you. Even Jesus did not always experience immediate healing when He invoked a miracle. In Luke 17:11-14, ten lepers were not healed immediately, but as they returned home. In Mark 8:22-26, Jesus had to heal a blind man twice before he could see. While this was not due to Jesus lacking authority over Satan, healing can be hindered by a lack of complete understanding on our part, by our lack of faith, and other reasons. Remember to call on the name of Jesus when you pray.

2. Have you considered the cost of moving from knowing Jesus

to being a sold-out, fully committed, passionate follower of Jesus? What are some personal costs to you?

Memory Verse:

2 Corinthians 5:20 *"We are therefore Christ's ambassadors, as though God were making his appeal through us."*

Evangelism

You have an important role in bringing others to Christ. Habakkuk 2:14 tells us that someday, *"The earth will be filled with the knowledge of the glory of the Lord, as the waters cover the sea."* We are given the awesome privilege of participating in that vision. But some people will say, "I'm sorry, I'm not called to do that." Or, "God can do it all by Himself; He doesn't need my help." But God was clear that He wants our participation in bringing others to Christ. We are called by Jesus to be witnesses of what He has done to change our lives (Acts 1:8), to go out into the world and preach the gospel (Mark 16:15), and to make disciples, or followers of Jesus (Matthew 28:19). In fact, the last two were Jesus' final instructions to his disciples. In John 15:16, Jesus said, *"...I chose you and appointed you to go and bear fruit—fruit that will last."* Yes, God could do it all by Himself, but by His design He chooses to work through us.

Key Principle: You work in partnership with the Holy Spirit to lead others to Christ.[17]

The Holy Spirit has a specific role and you have an equally important role in leading others to Christ. First, His role is to woo people to Christ. If you are alert to the opportunity to cooperate with the Holy Spirit, He will bring these people He is wooing across your path. Next comes your role, to tell others what Jesus has done in your life, to be a witness. In order to do this, you need to be sensitive to opportunities to direct your conversation toward spiritual matters. Then comes His role, to soften their heart so that they can allow Jesus to impact their lives. Be aware that while you are giving your testimony, or telling about Jesus' death on the cross, He will take your words and make them pierce the heart of the person you are trying to reach. Do not worry about stumbling while you are telling your story. The Holy Spirit will work supernaturally to ensure your words will make an impact. Finally, your role is to encourage them to invite Jesus into their lives, lead them in prayer to accept Jesus, assure them of their salvation, and encourage them to get in the word.

We have to be alert to the opportunity to be a witness. When people are gathered around the television watching the Super Bowl is not a particularly good time to start a spiritual conversation. A better time is when you have one-to-one face time with no distractions, in the home of someone who just heard he has cancer, in a coffee shop with someone who is struggling in a relationship, in a church with someone who is grieving, in a jail with someone who is wondering what the rest of his life will look like, in a nursing home with someone who only sees death in her future, in a hospital room with someone who desperately needs healing, or on an airplane with someone who is just killing time. Always ask permission to share something that has made a difference in your life. If you keep in mind that you are partnering with the Holy Spirit and are not doing this on your own, you will be amazed to witness a transformation in lives as the Holy Spirit softens hearts and opens minds. You should always offer to lead the person in a prayer of salvation, before the person walks away and the window of opportunity closes.

Jesus said in John 15:5, *"I am the vine; you are the branches. If a man remains in me and I in him, he will bear much fruit; apart from me you can do nothing."* When we stay in close fellowship with Jesus, we can begin to be fruitful for the kingdom of God.

That is Satan's greatest fear concerning you, that you will become fruitful, and that you will reproduce. Now you are taking the battle to the enemy. If you have not been walking closely with Jesus, then you need to humbly come back to Him. Joel 2:12 says, *"Return to me with all your heart, with fasting and weeping and mourning"* until fellowship is restored and any hindrances are removed.

APPLICATION:

1. Leading someone to Christ
   a. He/she should first understand that we are all sinners and so we need a savior. If they have trouble understanding that, ask them if they would like to take a test to see how they stack up. The test is the Ten Commandments. Then ask if he has ever lied, stolen, coveted something of his neighbor's, committed adultery, or used the Lord's name in vain.
   b. Explain that under the law of sin and death mentioned in Romans 8:2, he/she is deserving of death, or eternal separation from God (Romans 6:23a).
   c. Explain how God made a way out of this predicament so we do not have to die (Romans 5:8). Jesus took our death penalty upon Himself.
   d. Let him/her know that God desires that we come back to Him in an attitude of repentance, desiring to change our lifestyle.
   e. By receiving Jesus' free gift, he/she can become a child of God (John 1:12). He/she can receive the gift by praying a simple prayer. Offer to lead the person in a prayer where he/she confesses the lordship of Jesus in his/her own life (Romans 10:9). Remember that by proclaiming his/her belief before witnesses, he is establishing in heaven and on earth that he is under God's authority.
   f. After he prays the prayer of salvation, share some verses. In Luke 12:8, Jesus said, *"I tell you, whoever acknowledges me before men, the Son of Man will also acknowledge him before the angels of God."* Luke 15:10 says, *"...I tell*

you, there is rejoicing in the presence of the angels of God over one sinner who repents."

2. Do not underestimate the power of sharing from God's word. Romans 1:16 says, *"It is the power of God for the salvation of everyone who believes."*

3. Do not be discouraged if your discussion does not produce results. It is our job to plant seeds and water them and the Holy Spirit's job to reap the harvest. Even when your discussion seems fruitless, you have planted a seed. 1 Corinthians 15:58 says, *"Your labor in the Lord is not in vain."*

4. There are some places where it is easy to share the gospel: jail, hospital, nursing home, or disaster site. These people need God's love, and they are not going anywhere, so you have plenty of time to talk to them.

5. As your reward for being obedient to God's command to share the gospel, the prophet Daniel gives the following promise (Daniel 12:3): *"Those who are wise will shine like the brightness of the heavens, and those who lead many to righteousness, like the stars for ever and ever."*

6. Who do you know in your sphere of influence who is not saved? Will you pray for them regularly?

Memory Verse:

Luke 9:26 *"If anyone is ashamed of me and my words, the Son of Man will be ashamed of him when he comes in his glory and in the glory of the Father and of the holy angels."*

Holy Living

Paul talked about living a holy life in a letter to Titus. In Titus 2:11-12, he said, *"For the grace of God that brings salvation has appeared to all men. It teaches us to say 'No' to ungodliness and worldly passions, and to live self-controlled, upright, and godly lives in this present age."* The fact that God forgives our sins does not give us the license to go on sinning. We are to live godly lives. What are the worldly passions that Paul refers to? We find an answer in 1 John 2:16. *"For everything in the world—the cravings of sinful man* (materialism and selfishness), *the lust of his eyes* (sexual lust, greed, and envy), *and the boasting of what he has and does* (pride and arrogance)—*comes not from the Father but from the world."* Only God's grace, given to us through the Holy Spirit, can produce holy living in us. When we willfully choose to continue living in sin (sexual immorality, materialism brought on by greed and pride, dishonesty, feeding addictions instead of getting help, slandering others and passing judgment, using coarse language) we are fighting the Holy Spirit who is at work in us to make us holy. Just because the world is doing it does not make it acceptable. *"Therefore come out from them and be separate, says the Lord. Touch no unclean thing, and I will receive you. I will be a Father to you, and you will be my sons and daughters, says the Lord Almighty"* (2 Corinthians 6:17-18). God wants us to be separate from the world. His intention, according to Titus 2:14, is *"to purify for himself a people that are his very own, eager to do what is good."* Don't you love the fact that God looks down on you and says, "There's one of my very special people. He works hard to cooperate with the Holy Spirit in order to stay pure. He stands ready to be my servant when I need him." In 2 Timothy 2:20-21, Paul says the following, *"In a large house there are articles not only of gold and silver, but also of wood and clay; some are for noble purposes and some for ignoble. If a man cleanses himself from the latter, he will be an instrument for noble purposes, made holy, useful to the Master and prepared to do any good work."* If we clean up the impure stuff in our lives, God will use us to be His instrument for good in someone else's life. Oh, what a promise! If we are willing to become pure and live Godly lives, we will enjoy intimacy with the Father, and we will be used to carry out His will on this earth.

APPLICATION:

1. What impure stuff is in your house, in your life? Where do you need to clean house? *"Search me, O God, and know my heart; test me and know my anxious thoughts. See if there is any offensive way in me, and lead me in the way everlasting"* (Psalm 139:24).

2. Look, there is not some level of holiness you must achieve before God will love you. He has always loved you. But He wants to purify you now, both to use you as his shining light in the world and to get you ready to live with Him in His perfect heavenly kingdom. So will you examine yourself with an eye toward allowing the Holy Spirit to change you?

3. Will you confess your impurities to God? ("Yes, Lord, you know what I'm like, I can't hide it from you.") and ask the Holy Spirit to help you clean house ("God, I am willing to be purified, like gold in the refiner's fire. Have your way with me, Lord.")

Memory Verse:

2 Corinthians 6:17b-18 *"Touch no unclean thing, and I will receive you. I will be a Father to you, and you will be my sons and daughters, says the Lord Almighty."*

Becoming Like Christ

We are told in 2 Corinthians 3:18 that we *" . . . are being transformed into his likeness with ever-increasing glory."* Our goal, therefore, during our time on earth, should be to become like Christ. This is not something that happens immediately when you are saved, but may take a lifetime to accomplish. Think of it as a work in progress, where you become more like Him a little bit at a time. In John 13:15, Jesus said, *"I have set you an example that you should do as I have done for you."* It is worth our time to study the example Jesus set for us while on the earth. Several of these we have already talked about.

Jesus was holy.

Jesus laid hands on the sick.

Jesus continually served others.

Jesus had a prayer life and talked to the Father every day.

Jesus had compassion for peoples' needs. (See Mark 8:2.) When God's love fills our heart, we become less worried about our own needs and more concerned about others' needs.

Jesus brought light into the world. In Matthew 5:14, He said, *"You are the light of the world."* He passed the torch to us and expects us to be that light. During the Sermon on the Mount, Jesus instructed us that our light should shine in such a way that we bring glory to God. *"In the same way, let your light shine before men, that they may see your good deeds and praise your Father in heaven."* (Matthew 5:16.)

Jesus brought glory to God through His life's work. He understood and carried out the Father's plan for His life. In John 17:4, Jesus said, *"I have completed the work that you gave me to do. I have glorified you on the earth."*

Jesus suffered. In John 15:20, Jesus said, *"If they persecuted me, they will persecute you also."* 1 Peter 4:13 says, *"But rejoice that you participate in the sufferings of Christ."*

Jesus worked to oppose Satan. 1 John 3:8 says, *"The reason the son of God appeared was to destroy the devil's work."* The devil is still at large in the world and our job is not to avoid (or ignore) the evil in the world, but to fight it.

Jesus did not condemn sinners He encountered. John 3:17 says, *"For God did not send his Son into the world to condemn the world, but to save the world through him."* It is our job to disclose the truth of the gospel to the lost of this world, not to expose the sins of men and condemn them or be judgmental toward them.

APPLICATION:

1. Wow, if I'm to become like Christ, I have a lot of changing to do. In what areas are you most like Christ? In what areas are you least like Christ?
2. In your time alone with God, try to not pray a single prayer for yourself but pray for others' needs.

3. What can you do to shine the light of Christ's love in your church or community? Does the fear of persecution cause you to hide your light from the world?

4. In John 15:1-2, Jesus said, *"I am the true vine, and my Father is the gardener. He cuts off every branch in me that bears no fruit, while every branch that does bear fruit he prunes so that it will be even more fruitful."* So if we are abiding in Jesus, and vitally connected to Him, we will be learning to walk like Jesus walked. God the Father will be cultivating our vine, cutting away our dead branches and pruning the live ones so they produce fruit, not just leaves. He directs the lives of believers into fruitful activity. Will pruning be painful? Not if we cooperate. God will place before us opportunities to bear fruit; the Holy Spirit will speak softly that this is where we are to go; our Christian brothers and sisters will invite us to participate with them in fruitful ministries. And if we choose to obey God's calling, we will produce fruit. But Jesus warns in John 15:6, *"If anyone does not remain in me, he is like a branch that is thrown away and withers; such branches are picked up, thrown into the fire and burned."* As we learned in 1 Corinthians 3:13-14, God tests the quality of our deeds with fire.

5. How do you know when your life's work is complete? Is Jesus ruling from His throne on earth yet? Then it is not complete.

6. If we are to imitate Christ, we should be destroying the devil's work. When you mentor a young man who has no father and give him a vision for his life, when you help an addict to stay on the road to recovery, when you visit a sick person and pray for his healing in the name of Jesus, when you visit a jail and tell an inmate about the gospel of Jesus Christ, when you disciple a new believer and help her to become mature in her faith, when you fight injustice in the world, and when you combat hunger and homelessness, you are fighting the devil. You are hitting him where he lives. You are opposing him and

keeping him in check. If all Christians did more to combat the devil, this world would be a radically different place. *"Do not be overcome by evil, but overcome evil with good"* (Romans 12:21.)

7. What are you doing to consciously avoid condemning someone who is not as Godly as you? Do you look at that person and feel superior?

8. What is God calling you to change in your life in order to become like Christ? Record it in the appendix.

Memory Verse:

1 John 2:6 *"Whoever claims to live in him must walk as Jesus did."*

Dealing with Tragedy

Christians are not exempt from tough times. In John 16:33b, Jesus said, *"In this world you will have trouble. But take heart! I have overcome the world."*

Why Does God Allow Suffering?

First, you should know that God does not cause suffering. There are no instances in the New Testament of Jesus' inflicting pain, causing people to get sick, causing a natural disaster to happen, or causing a deadly accident to occur. Hebrews 1:3 says, *"The Son is the radiance of God's glory and the exact representation of his being."* So if Jesus is the exact representation of God and Jesus never inflicts suffering on people, then neither does God. So that's settled.

But God does at times permit the evil in the world to impact us, and that evil is all around us. He has legitimate reasons for permitting it to happen. He lifts His hedge of protection for just a minute and something out of the ordinary hits us. And the Bible tells us to expect it. We are not immune to it because we are Christians. So how does God want us to deal with suffering and what can we learn from it?

There are several reasons something bad may happen to you.

One reason is that God may be disciplining you. Hebrews 12:10 says, *"God disciplines us for our good, that we may share in his holiness."* Of course we do not like to think we have done something to merit God's punishment, until a Christian brother asks, "How's your relationship with God?" right after disaster strikes. Then you begin to ask yourself if God is trying to tell you that you have not been spending enough time with Him. If you think this could be the reason, then your first response should be confession and asking forgiveness.

Secondly, God may want you to learn to rely on Him more, and be a bit less self-reliant. Give your suffering to God and ask God to walk with you through the whole ordeal. *"God has said, 'Never will I leave you; never will I forsake you.'"* (Hebrews 13:5).

Thirdly, God may want you to develop compassion and learn to help others going through the same experience. Ask God to bring friends alongside you to show you how to minister to others, and when disaster strikes, to help you to be the hands of feet of Jesus to someone else. Remember how you felt when friends came by to bring you a meal, or give you a card, or just ask how you were doing, or someone who had been through the same ordeal came by to tell you what to expect or how to get through it. Then do the same for others. 2 Corinthians 1:3-4 says, *"Praise be to the God and Father of our Lord Jesus Christ, the Father of compassion and the God of all comfort, who comforts us in all our troubles, so that we can comfort those in any trouble with the comfort we ourselves have received from God."*

Next, maybe like Job, Satan has asked God for permission to test you. "Sure, that guy praises You now, but haven't You blessed his socks off? Stretch out your hand to strike him and see if he doesn't curse You." If you think this could be the reason, then ask God to strengthen your faith and to help you proclaim His praises throughout the ordeal. Offer up praise to God when you ask for prayers of healing, when you give updates on your situation, and when He delivers you. Consider that many people turn away from God when they experience horrible suffering. "If there was a God, He wouldn't have allowed my child to die," they might exclaim. Remember the promise of James 1:12, *"Blessed is the man who perseveres under trial, because when he has stood the test, he will receive the crown of life that God has promised to those who love him."*

Next, maybe God is just helping you to become mature. If this could be the reason, ask God to help you rejoice through your sufferings. Romans 5:3-4 says, *"But we also rejoice in our sufferings, because we know that suffering produces perseverance; perseverance, character; and character, hope."* Another reason for rejoicing is because your faith, throughout the ordeal, has proved genuine. 1 Peter 1:7 says, when speaking of suffering through trials, *"These have come so that your faith—of greater worth than gold, which perishes even though refined by fire—may be proved genuine and may result in praise, glory and honor when Jesus Christ is revealed."*

Finally, maybe God wants you to break an unhealthy habit. Yes some of the suffering we bring upon ourselves is the result of our own poor decisions or addictive behavior. Pray to God for strength to change your behavior and then seek help.

Remember to thank God when the trial is over.

APPLICATION:

1. How can God be glorified when you are going through a difficult ordeal? Keep your friends appraised of what is going on with you, and ask them to pray for you. If your church has a prayer chain, publicize your prayer request. Give God thanks privately and publicly for every little victory along the way. Let others know you are trusting in God for healing and recovery. Thank your friends who dropped by, sent cards, delivered meals, and offered encouragement, for lifting your spirits. If the days ahead get darker, tell your friends you are continuing to trust in God and that He has not abandoned you. When the ordeal is over, regardless of whether the outcome met your expectations, thank those in your prayer chain who prayed with you, your friends who stood by you, and your God who stayed beside you.

2. When others are going through difficult times, you can bring

glory to God by being the hands and feet of Christ. You can visit the person and pray for him/her. If there is illness, you can do the messy work of changing a dressing, or emptying a bedpan or catheter bag. You can help others get caught up on their housework, make a meal, run an errand, mow their lawn. Mail cards, text encouragement, inject some humor. Will you make the effort to be the hands and feet of Christ to someone who is suffering?

3. God is able to turn every bad situation around and use it for good. Will you ask Him to make something positive come from your situation?

Memory Verse:

John 16:33b *"In this world you will have trouble. But take heart! I have overcome the world."*

Week 6

The End Times

Read Matthew 24:3-44

Jesus spoke in this passage about the end times. This is a period of great tribulation and distress, during which a world dictator known as the Antichrist will come to power. Following this, Jesus will return to conquer all evil in the world. Verse 21 tells us the tribulation will be a period of great distress <u>unlike the world has ever seen</u> or will ever see again. This means, in terms of public health, it will be worse than the era of the Black Plague. Economically speaking, it will be worse than the Great Depression. In terms of war, it will be worse than the World Wars. In terms of persecution, it will be worse than the Holocaust. Because of so much wickedness, the Bible says the love of most will grow cold (verse 12). Jesus said in verse 36 that no one knows the day or the hour when the tribulation will come, not even Jesus himself. But He did say in verses 32-33 that you can know the season and observe the signs of its pending arrival. In verse 33, He said, *"When you see all these things, you know that it is near, right at the door."* In verse 8, He described the end times as coming on like birth pains. For those who have never experienced childbirth, contractions come on slowly at first; then they increase in frequency and intensity. Likewise, all the signs that Jesus talked about (famines, earthquakes, wars, pestilence, wickedness, believers turning away from their faith, persecution of believers, the appearance of false prophets, and, cosmic disturbances) will increase in frequency and intensity as the return of Jesus comes closer.

If you Google "earthquake frequency," you will find charts that clearly show earthquakes are increasing in frequency and intensity. If you consider the threats to the world's health over the last several years (H1N1 swine flu, H5N1 avian flu, SARS, mad cow, H7N9 avian flu, and West Nile virus) you know that pestilence is on the rise. Look to the Middle East and you will see violent revolution breaking out in many countries, and the threat of pending war. As to religious persecution, it ranges from subtle attacks, such as attempts to remove God from our society, to more personal attacks, such as portraying someone who believes Jesus is the only way as intolerant of other religions. In many nations, Christians are undergoing extreme persecution, such as imprisonment and murder. Economically, the world had a taste of impending calamity during the 2008 recession. Today many countries are on the verge of bankruptcy and financial collapse. Consider the 2004 Indonesian tsunami and the 2011 Japanese tsunami. Jesus said that nations would be in anguish at the roaring and tossing of the sea (Luke 21:35). These signs are certainly pointing to the end times, but this is not to say that this is the only time in history that the end times were approaching. There have been numerous times in history when conditions looked bleak, but the people humbled themselves, repented of their sin, and asked God to heal their land. The Bible says, in 2 Chronicles 7:14, that if we do the same, our day of judgment will be postponed.

Other Prophecies Concerning the End Times Are as Follows:

Just before Jesus' crucifixion, He predicted that Jerusalem would be destroyed (Matthew 24:2) and the nation scattered. This prophecy came true less than 40 years after Jesus departed the earth. For nearly 1900 years, the Jews were scattered around the world and persecuted throughout history. In 1948, the nation of Israel was formed and Jews from around the world returned to their homeland. The creation of the Jewish nation is significant because Jesus prophesied that the Antichrist will one day war against the nation of Israel (Matthew 24:15-19).

Prophecies Not Yet Fulfilled

Paul mentioned, in 2 Thessalonians 2:4, that the Antichrist would set himself up in God's temple and proclaim that he is God. Jesus and the prophet Daniel called this "the abomination that causes desolation" (Matthew 24:15, Daniel 9:27). At this time in history, Jews in Israel are making plans to rebuild the temple. According to the Law of Moses, the temple will be built to the exact specifications delineated in the Old Testament. It is Israel's desire that the temple stand on Mount Moriah, the site of the first two temples. Unfortunately, the Dome of the Rock, one of Islam's most sacred sites, sits squarely on top of the old temple site. Watch to see how this plays out.

Jesus mentioned in Matthew 24:14 that *"This gospel of the kingdom will be preached in the whole world as a testimony to all nations, and then the end will come." Revelation 5:9 mentions that Heaven will consist of people from every tribe and language and people and nation.* So every people group will have a chance to hear the gospel before the end comes. The age of the internet and wireless communication will make this a reality sometime during this decade. Watch for the gospel to spread like wildfire.

The prophet Joel predicted a great outpouring of the Holy Spirit in the end days (Joel 2:28-30). For a picture of what that will look like, read the book of Acts, which tells of the role of the Holy Spirit in evangelizing the world in the first century. People will be able to hear the gospel preached in their own language (Acts 2:6). Thousands of new believers will be added in a single day (Acts 2:41). Many people will be healed of their infirmities or released from evil spirits (Acts 8:7). Entire cities will be saved (Acts 9:35). People will overcome intense persecution to ensure the gospel is spread to all people (Acts 14:19-20). Entire continents will hear the Word (Acts 19:10). It will truly be an exciting time in the life of every believer. Watch for an increase in miracles of the Holy Spirit. They are already happening in some countries.

APPLICATION:

1. We should not be surprised to see end time events start to unfold before our eyes. We will see steps to implement world government, if an Antichrist is to somehow take power. We will see natural disasters increase in frequency and intensity. We will increasingly see false prophets. And we will see people coming to Christ around the globe in a sweeping revival.

2. How should we prepare for the coming tribulation? We should prepare ourselves spiritually by purifying ourselves from the culture of the world and returning humbly to God. We should prepare ourselves emotionally for difficult times ahead and be looking to God for protection. We should prepare ourselves physically by getting in shape, getting our families prepared for disasters, and being prepared to be the hands and feet of Christ to a hurting world when disaster strikes.

3. During these difficult times, people will want to know where is God in all of this. Will you be able to share God's plan to rescue those who love Him?

Memory Verse:

Matthew 24:33 *"Even so, when you see all these things, you know that it is near, right at the door."*

The Antichrist

Read Revelation chapter 13, and 2 Thessalonians 2:3-12.

The Antichrist is a world dictator who will suddenly come to power in the end times. He will be given the power to perform counterfeit miracles, signs, and wonders. He will rule the entire world with absolute power. He will proclaim himself to be God and demand that everyone worship him. God will cause many people to be mesmerized and deceived by this leader (2 Thessalonians 2:3-12).

The Antichrist will blaspheme Jesus. He will require all people to take his mark on their right hand or forehead in order to buy or sell anything. The number of the Antichrist is 666. He will make war against believers and many will be killed or put in prison for refusing to worship him.

He will mock the triune nature of God by having his own sort of triune leadership. There will be the world ruler, there will be a prophet who will exhort people to worship the world leader, and there will be the devil himself. The world leader will suffer a fatal wound but then the devil will inhabit his body and he will come back to life. The entire world will be astonished. The devil will finally have the power he has coveted since the creation of man.

His reign will be 7 years, according to the prophet Daniel. During the first 3½ years, he will make a treaty with Israel, possibly to permit Israel to rebuild the temple in Jerusalem. He will be a popular leader.

At the mid-point of his reign, he will enter the temple and declare himself to be God. Then the period of persecution against all those who refuse to worship him will begin. God warns us to not take his mark. *"There is no rest day or night for those who worship the beast and his image, or for anyone who receives the mark of his name"* (Revelation 14:11).

The bible speaks of a restrainer in 2 Thessalonians 2:5-9, who is holding back the secret power of lawlessness, the Antichrist. The restrainer is the church indwelled by the Holy Spirit. We are tasked with opposing the work of Satan on this earth. When the restrainer is removed, then the lawless one will be revealed. We will discuss in the next section how God will remove his church prior to the Antichrist being revealed.

During this 7-year reign, God will bring judgment upon the earth. The **"seal"** judgments will be spread out over most of the seven years and include the appearance of the Antichrist, cold war and alliances followed immediately by open conquest, famine, death (from war, famine, and plague), persecution of believers, and cosmic disturbances in the sky (see Revelation 6). Near the end of Satan's seven-year reign, the **"trumpet"** judgments will occur, packed together in a shorter time period and with much more intensity. These will be God's judgment against the earth. Volcanic eruptions and comets striking the earth will poison the oceans, rivers, and lakes. There will be increased demonic activity. Next, a third of mankind will be killed by plagues of fire, smoke, and sulfur (see Revelation 8 and 9). All of these judgments will be proclaimed as coming from God, with God calling on all people to repent and turn to Him. Finally, God's patience will wear out and the time for turning to Jesus will end. Any remaining believers who are still alive will be delivered from the earth (see Revelation 11:15-18, 1 Corinthians 15:52, and Revelation 14: 14-15) and then God will bring the final "**bowl**" judgments against those who are still mocking God (see Revelation 16). This will conclude with the battle of Armageddon, (on the plains of Meggido in Israel) where Jesus will come back as a warrior. Jesus will be accompanied by all the saints from throughout the ages, and He will bring death to those who refused to repent and acknowledge Him (Revelation 19:11-21). Satan will be captured during the battle of Armageddon and locked up in the abyss (see Revelation 20:1-3). Then Jesus will reign on earth for a thousand years with all the saints who were martyred for Christ. At the end of the thousand years, Satan will be released from prison and go out to try to deceive the nations once again. Satan will be captured and thrown into the lake of fire, where he will be tormented day and night forever. Finally, God will create a new heaven and a new earth and will live with His people forever in the New Jerusalem.

APPLICATION:

1. Did you ever wonder why Satan doesn't give in and surrender to God? Surely he has read of his fate in Revelation 20:1-3. It has to be because Satan believes he can win. He believes that, through sheer numbers, he can defeat Jesus and the saints as they show up at Armageddon to put an end to the evil in the world. That is why he is now desperate to add to his numbers. He has accumulated an impressive army of his own followers; he is deceiving believers with false religions; he is trying to remove all mention of God from the earth; and he has made Christ's followers ineffective by diverting their attention from doing God's work to living for themselves. But praise God, everything in the Bible has to come true just as it is written. In Revelation 19:11-16, Jesus is shown returning as a warrior, with eyes blazing like fire, a tattoo on His thigh, crowns on His head, with blood on his robe, riding a white horse. Out of his mouth comes a sharp sword, which strikes down every one of Satan's followers. Riding behind Jesus are all the saints. Satan and his false prophet will be captured and locked up. Do you envision yourself as a warrior for Jesus Christ?

2. Why will it take so long to happen? This question was being asked by the church nearly 2000 years ago. 2 Peter 3:9 says,

"The Lord is not slow in keeping his promise, as some understand slowness. He is patient with you, not wanting anyone to perish, but everyone to come to repentance." So God has been patient with man, despite all the evil in the world, in order that more people would have a chance to hear the gospel. But God will not give man a chance to repent forever. Revelation 15:8 describes a period between the 7 trumpet judgments and the final 7 bowl judgments where no one can enter God's temple, no one can approach God's mercy seat, until the final judgments are delivered. This is the point where God's patience finally runs out. There are no more chances to repent after that.

3. Are you doing the work that Jesus did, opposing the work of the devil? Satan is restrained when you take a stand against injustice, help feed the hungry, pray for the sick, help someone rebuild from a disaster, visit the lonely, come alongside someone who has an addiction and help them in their journey toward wholeness, or share the gospel.

Memory Verse:

2 Thessalonians 3:3 *"But the Lord is faithful, and he will strengthen and protect you from the evil one."*

The Rapture

Read Luke 12:35-40.

Will believers somehow be spared the pain of the tribulation period? Yes, God provides a way out for those who are "true" believers in Jesus. God is always so good to those who truly love Him. While the word "Rapture" is not found in the bible, the event, being "caught up" is. And that's what the word Rapture means, to be caught up.

1 Thessalonians 4:16,17 describes the event. *"For the Lord himself will come down from heaven, with a loud command, with the voice of the archangel and with the trumpet call of God, and the dead in Christ will rise first. After that, we who are still alive and are left will be caught up together with them in the clouds to meet the Lord in the air. And so we will be with the Lord forever."* Bible scholars disagree on when it will actually take place. But we do know this, *"The Son of Man will come at an hour when you do not expect him,"* (Luke 12:40). Jesus warned us to be always ready, (emotionally, spiritually, and physically) and to be dressed to serve (Luke 12:35). His desire is that the believer will not be overcome by the distress of the end times. Instead, the believer will be ministering to those who are experiencing the pain of those troubling times leading up to and during the tribulation. He will be a beacon of light in the darkness. Jesus' church should be a showcase of His love to the world, and thus be a witness to those in the world who do not know Jesus.

In Luke 21:34 Jesus said, *"Be careful, or your hearts will be weighed down with dissipation, drunkenness and the anxieties of life, and that day* (the day of Jesus' return for His church) *will close on you unexpectedly like a trap."* This verse suggests Jesus's return for His church will come at a time when many peoples' lives are crashing in on them, when they are experiencing those birth pains mentioned previously. 1 Corinthians 15:52 tells us it will happen *"in a flash, in the twinkling of an eye."* Since God never forces anything upon you, you will most likely have a split second to decide if you are going. Now is not the time to call your unsaved friend and share the gospel with him. Now is not the time to call your business partner and tell him how to finish that project you were working. Now is not the time to stop and feed the dog. Part of being ready is to be completely un-chained to this world and ready to leave with Jesus *" . . . so that when he comes and knocks they can immediately open the door for him"* (Luke 12:36b).

APPLICATION:

1. Are you ready for Christ's return, or are you too caught up in the culture of the world? Matthew 24:42-44 says, *"Therefore keep watch, because you do not know on what day your Lord will come. But understand this: If the owner of the house had known at what time of night the thief was coming, he would have kept watch and would not have let his house be broken into. So you also must be ready, because the Son of Man will come at an hour when you do not expect him."* Remember, the church will already have been raptured when the Antichrist is finally revealed (see 2 Thessalonians 2:7-8).

2. If God's angel appeared in your bedroom tonight, would you be ready to go? *If not, why not?*

Memory Verse:

Luke 12:40 *"You also must be ready, because the Son of Man will come at an hour when you do not expect him."*

Left Behind

Will some believers be left behind during the Rapture? Apparently, that is the case with the ones who are not "true" believers. Matthew 24:40-41 says, *"Two men will be in the field; one will be taken and the other left. Two women will be grinding with a hand mill; one will be taken and the other left."* The ones left behind are those who may have had head knowledge of Jesus but did not have Him in their hearts and were not surrendered to Him.

Further clarification of what a "true" believer looks like can be found in the letters to the seven churches, in the book of Revelation.

The Letters to the 7 Churches
Read Revelation chapters 2 and 3, the letters to the seven churches.

In these chapters, Jesus sends messages to seven of the early churches to tell them what He likes and dislikes about each of them. Jesus was talking to the church, not to the unbelieving world. This is confirmed by the statement at the close of each letter that the Spirit was speaking to the churches (chapter 2, verse 7, 11, 17, 29, and chapter 3, verse 6, 13, 22). Some Bible scholars argue that these letters only apply to those individual churches, some 2000 years ago. But others will say that since they are part of the book (Revelation) that discusses the end times, they apply to today's church as well. Since the number seven represents God's completeness, these seven churches could be interpreted to mean seven sets of conditions being experienced by the one church of Jesus Christ. Regardless, since God does not change through the ages, things that displeased God then still displease Him now, and things that pleased God back then still please Him now. By analyzing the seven messages, we can paint a picture of the kind of life that is totally pleasing to God, that is, the "true" believer.

The Traits That Are Pleasing to God

- Ephesus: worked hard for the Kingdom, didn't tolerate wicked men, were committed to the truth
- Smyrna: were rich (generous) toward God even though they had little
- Pergamum: remained true to their faith despite enduring persecution
- Thyatira: were doing more good deeds through love, faith, service, and perseverance
- Sardis: remained pure despite the evil times
- Philadelphia: did not deny His name, even in the face of persecution
- Laodicea: there was nothing pleasing to God about this church

The Traits That Are Displeasing to God

- Ephesus: had forsaken their first love, no longer passionate about Jesus
- Smyrna: some were slandering others in the church to stir up dissension
- Pergamum: condoned the teaching of Balaam: sexual immorality, idolatry, worshipping false gods
- Thyatira: tolerated false prophets, false religions
- Sardis: once were alive but had become spiritually dead, had not completed the ministry God gave them to do, had no good deeds to show for themselves
- Philadelphia: no faults were found with this church

- Laodicea: lukewarm, wealthy but spiritually poor, their witness was worthless (because they lived like the rest of the
world), found security in wealth rather than in God, were not
passionate about Him. Jesus invited them, even though they
were already presumed to be believers, to have a personal
relationship with Him.

Revelation 3:10 provides the key verse to understanding who will
be spared the tribulation. He said to the Philadelphians, the church
with whom he found no fault, *"Since you have kept my command
to endure patiently, I will also <u>keep you from the hour of trial</u> that is
going to come upon the whole world <u>to test</u> those who live on the
earth."* Remember, these letters were written to the seven churches.
Jesus is talking to believers here, not those who are unsaved.

Key Principle: Only those Christians whose lives are totally pleasing to God (it was the Philadelphians in this example) will be spared the test of the tribulation.

It makes perfect sense. If the tribulation period is a test for believers (as well as a last call for the unsaved), and the Philadelphians
were already pleasing God with their witness, their intense passion for
Jesus, their faithfulness, their bravery in the face of persecution, their
holding to sound doctrine, their good deeds, their generosity, their
keeping of the commandments, and their pure lives in an otherwise
evil world, then why would they have to stand the test again? It is only
the believers who are found lacking in some area who will be tested
by having to endure the tribulation period. Those who are tested and
overcome can still join in Heaven with those who were raptured. They
will be given the *"right to eat from the tree of life"* (Revelation 2:7),
"will not be hurt at all by the second death" (Revelation 2:11), will be
given *"a new name"* (Revelation 2:17), will be given *"authority over
the nations"* (Revelation 2:26), will be *"dressed in white"* (Revelation
3:4), will be a *"pillar in the temple of my God"* (Revelation 3:12), and
will *"sit with me on my throne"* (Revelation 3:21).

APPLICATION:

1. Let's look at the traits of the seven churches and study those things that please and displease God. The church at Ephesus did not tolerate wicked men. Does the world call on us to tolerate any wickedness today? Are Christians brainwashed into blending in and not standing out? What would sexual purity look like in these evil days? Do you ever slander others in your church? Have you idolized anyone in the music, sports, and entertainment industries? Is your Jesus the Son of God or just another angelic-like creation of God? What good deeds do you have to show as evidence that you are a follower of Jesus? Does your security lie in your retirement account or in God?

2. Why would God test us? Doesn't He already know how we will respond? It is so we might know what is in our hearts and repent and return to Him. [18] If you have progressed this far in the book, you have already had opportunities to examine whether you are living sold-out for Jesus or living with one foot in this world and one foot in His kingdom. Will you ask God to help you to be sold-out for Jesus, to bring you alongside other believers who are on fire, and to be fully devoted to Him?

Memory Verse:

Revelation 3:10 *"Since you have kept my command to endure patiently, I will also keep you from the hour of trial that is going to come upon the whole world to test those who live on the earth."*

Flameout

Read Matthew 25: 1-13, the parable of the ten virgins.

This parable describes a Jewish wedding in the time of Christ. The actual ceremony would go on for several days. The bride would be made ready by her bridesmaids (the ten virgins), and the groom would be attended to by his groomsmen, possibly at a bachelor-party-like remembrance of his single days. Then the groom and his attendants would make the trip to the bride's house, go through the religious ceremony, and the entire party would return to the groom's house to celebrate.

While it was not uncommon to run out of wine at a wedding (remember that is the reason Jesus turned water into wine), it would be inexcusable to run out of oil for the lamps. The parable describes five bridesmaids who were foolish; they either were totally unprepared and had no oil or were partially prepared and ran out of oil. When the groom came for his bride, he took with him the bridesmaids who had burning lamps, and he left behind the ones who did not. When the left-behind bridesmaids asked to borrow some oil, they were told to buy some for themselves. Why did they let their lamps run out? Could it be they were not expecting the groom's return? Were they stingy in how much oil they bought originally? Or were they just careless?

The groom in this story is Jesus. His return is represented by the Rapture and He is coming to claim His bride, His church. Those in the wedding party whose lamps are burning brightly (anticipating Christ's return, fully prepared, purifying their lives through holy living, passionate about serving Jesus, giving generously to the Kingdom, and telling others about Jesus) will go with the groom to His place to enjoy the wedding supper of the Lamb. Those whose lamps have gone out (holding back their devotion to Jesus, being stingy with their money and their service to Him, and not giving their all) will be left behind.

APPLICATION:

1. Do you know any Christians whose flames have gone out? Maybe they were once attending church faithfully, participating in Bible study or community groups, studying God's word, and sharing their testimony. Now they are caught up in the world, and have not been seen inside a church in years. Their passion for Jesus, once ablaze, has been snuffed out. As the parable explains, these people will not be returning with Jesus during the rapture. The story does not say they are destined for hell, but they will have to endure the tribulation period as a test of their true devotion. Only he who endures to the end will be saved.

2. It is interesting to note that five out of the ten were not permitted into the banquet room. Is Jesus trying to give us a glimpse into what percentage of people who claim to be believers will be left behind?

Memory Verse:

Matthew 24:40 *"Two men will be in the field; one will be taken and the other left."*

Being Sold-Out for Jesus

Reread Revelation 3:14-22 the letter to the church at Laodicea.

This passage is Jesus' harshest rebuke to His church. Jesus gives a warning, in Revelation 3:16, to those believers who are not passionate for Him. *"Because you are lukewarm—neither hot nor cold—I am about to spit you out of my mouth."* What caused this attitude? Wealth. Many Bible scholars say this is the letter directed to the church in America today. We have security in wealth, and we don't need to rely on God for anything. Some of us may even say, "I guess I am lukewarm," but, sadly, we do not really care to do anything about it. Jesus said we should buy gold refined in the fire. What currency can we use to buy anything from God? What do we have that God wants? He wants our full devotion. He wants us to place Him first and foremost in our lives. Then we can begin to empty ourselves of our love of self. He wants us to have an eternal perspective. Then we can purify our hearts from lusting after things of this world. He wants us to give our entire lives to serving Him. Then we can change our selfish ways. In Revelation 3:20, Jesus is standing at the entrance to our hearts, knocking, and waiting. Only by taking the step to opening the door and inviting Him in can we then begin to have a new relationship with Him.

Living a Life Sold-Out for Jesus

As the previous passage depicts, Jesus wants followers who are completely sold-out for Him. Reviewing the seven letters to the seven churches paints a pretty clear picture of what Jesus is looking for in His followers. He wants us to be telling others about Him and not backing down in the face of persecution from those in the world who are anti-Jesus. He wants us to be true to His word and not get sucked in to religions and philosophies where men lay out ideas that are counter to the Bible or lay on us additional requirements. He wants us to live holy lives and not be engaged in sexual immorality, slander, rebelliousness, and the wickedness of the world. He wants us to demonstrate our love for Him by putting Him first in every area of our lives and worshipping Him passionately. He wants us to be rich in good deeds and sharing our possessions with the needy, rather than bowing to the idols of materialism, greed, and wealth.

Many people have a plan for being hugely successful in life. They want to enjoy a comfortable life style, have influence among their peers, and even leave a legacy in order to be remembered for what they accomplished in this world. Sadly, most do not have a clue how to make their life count for God, and they are willing to settle for mediocrity in this area of their lives. We must be constantly saying "Yes" to the Holy Spirit when He guides us in the way we should go. We must learn to trust in the power of the Holy Spirit and not rely on our own strength and our limited resources. We must be bold and unashamed of the gospel and passionate to share our testimony. We must be willing to put a limit on our lifestyle so we can be generous to those in need. In short, we must be slaves to Christ (you were bought at a great price), realizing that we were created to serve God and to bring Him glory. In Matthew 20:27, Jesus said, *"Whoever wants to be first must be your slave—just as the Son of Man did not come to be served, but to serve."* Start energizing your prayer life, search the scriptures with new zeal, and get into community with other believers who also want to be sold-out.

Conclusion

God first redeemed us from experiencing eternal separation from Him, then He fully equipped us with the Holy Spirit, then He transformed us. For what purpose? Was it so we can earn a living and enjoy all the comforts of life, or did He have something bigger in mind? God has a plan for your life that will give your life significance in this world and in His heavenly kingdom. We already discussed that we can begin to uncover that plan by saying "Yes" when He speaks to us. We learned that if we purify our lives, He will make us His instrument for doing good in this world. We learned the importance of loving God above everything else in our lives and having a relationship with God. We learned that loving others, especially the poor and lowly, is the best expression of our love for God. We learned that our enemy will attempt to derail us, but he no longer has any authority over us. Because we are under the authority of Jesus, we have authority over the enemy. Finally, we learned that the Holy Spirit will empower us with His grace to be so much more effective for God than we could ever be in our own strength.

We can see all around us the signs of the end times. We should be living in expectation of Jesus' imminent return for His church. It will not be long before God's mercy seat is closed. There is much work to be done to reach the lost for Christ. We should run the race that has been laid out for us. Do not participate in some haphazard, half-hearted fashion, but *"Run in such a way as to get the prize"* (1 Corinthians 9:24). Paul said, in Romans 2:7, that we should *"Seek glory, honor, and immortality"* by persistently doing good. We don't pursue glory for ourselves in this world, but when we carry out God's will, we will receive glory and honor in the next.

God has fully equipped us to run the race. Isaiah 54:17 says, *"No weapon forged against you will prevail,"* because we are under the protection of the all-powerful, Creator God of the universe.

Review what God has been speaking to you over the course of this study and what changes He has asked you to make in your life. Over the next year, try working on one change each month.

APPLICATION:

1. Ask God to connect you to other believers who are on fire for Him.
2. How can you simplify your lifestyle in order to have time and money for serving God?
3. In what direction do you feel God is currently leading you?
4. How can you energize your relationship with the Most High God?
5. In what areas do you need to disengage from the world?
6. Daily ask God to empty you of anything that is more important than He is. Surrender any sin you are still clinging to.
7. Periodically review the list you wrote in the appendix of things God is asking you to change. Are you changing?

Memory Verse:

Romans 12:1,2 *"Therefore, I urge you, brothers, in view of God's mercy, to offer your bodies as living sacrifices, holy and pleasing to God—this is your spiritual act of worship. Do not conform any longer to the pattern of this world, but be transformed by the renewing of your mind. Then you will be able to test and approve what God's will is—his good, pleasing and perfect will."*

Notes

1. Rick Warren, *The Purpose Driven Life*, Grand Rapids, Zondervan, 2002, page 17.
2. Francis Chan, "Just Stop and Think," www.youtube.com/watch?v=pRi4VwcrYmA .
3. Ibid.
4. Randy Alcorn, *Heaven*, Carol Stream, IL, Tyndale House, 2004, page 283.
5. C.S. Lovett, *Dealing With the Devil*, Baldwin Park, CA, Personal Christianity Chapel, 1967, page 89.
6. Charles Capps, *Your Spiritual Authority*, Tulsa, Harrison House, 1994, page 1.
7. John Bevere, *Extraordinary*, Colorado Springs, Waterbrook Press, 2009, page 143.
8. John Bevere, *Honor's Reward*, New York, Faith Words, 2007, page 104.
9. Isidore Agoha, *Demons are Subject to Us*, New York, 2007, page 45.
10. Ibid. page 50.
11. C.S. Lovett, *Dealing With the Devil*, Baldwin Park, CA, Personal Christianity Chapel, 1967, page 107.
12. Rick Warren, *The Purpose Driven Life*, Grand Rapids, Zondervan, 2002, page 42.
13. Henry and Richard Blackaby, *Hearing God's Voice*, Nashville, B&H Publishing Group, 2002, page 31.
14. Henry and Richard Blackaby, *Experiencing God*, Nashville, B&H Publishing Group, 2008, page 65.
15. *Crown Ministries*, Longwood, FL, Crown Ministries, 1995, page 39.
16. Benny Hinn, *The Annointing*, Nashville, Thomas Nelson, 1992, page 122.

17. John Bevere, *Drawing Near*, Nashville, Thomas Nelson, 2004, page 147.

18. John Bevere, *A Heart Ablaze*, Nashville, Thomas Nelson, 1999, page 48.

Appendix

List here new things you have discovered from the word of God, those things God is saying to you, and areas He is asking you to change.

New things I am discovering from the word of God:

_____

_____

_____

_____

_____

_____

_____

Things God is saying to me:

_____

_____

_____

_____

_____

_____

Things God is asking me to change:

_____

_____

_____

_____

_____

_____

CPSIA information can be obtained at www.ICGtesting.com
Printed in the USA
LVOW06s0332060614

388812LV00002B/100/P